REINVENTING YOURSELF

REINVENTING YOURSELF

A Metaphysical
Self-Renewal System

DICK SUTPHEN

Other Metaphysical Books By Dick Sutphen

(Simon & Schuster Pocket Books)

You Were Born Again To Be Together
Past Lives, Future Loves
Unseen Influences
Predestined Love
Finding Your Answers Within
Earthly Purpose
The Oracle Within

(Valley of the Sun Publishing)

Master of Life Manual
Enlightenment Transcripts
Lighting The Light Within
Past-Life Therapy In Action
Sedona: Psychic Energy Vortexes
Heart Magic
The Spiritual Path Guidebook

Also From Valley of the Sun

350+ audio/video tape titles:
Self-Help, Self-Exploration & Audio Books.
Master of Life Winners is a quarterly magazine mailed free.
Write for a copy.

First Edition: January 1993

Valley of the Sun Publishing, Box 38, Malibu CA 90265

ISBN Number 0-87554-499-1
Library of Congress Card Number 91-068564

ACKNOWLEDGEMENTS

Many thanks to all the writers, doctors, philosophers, and teachers who have influenced these communications—especially Lauren Leigh Meyer, Dr. David Viscott, Dr. William Glasser, Dr. Mihaly Csikszentmihalyi, Dr. Robert Anthony, Jennifer James, Ph.D., Paul Pearsall, Ph.D., David K. Reynolds, Ph.D., Alan Watts, Will Schultz, Jimmy Moore, J. Krishnamurti, Vernon Howard, Harry Browne, Frederic M. Hudson, Stewart Emery, Joe Hyams, Bhagwan Shree Rajneesh (Osho), and a few Zen Masters who crossed over long ago.

The Critical 13 were originally produced as an audio tape published by Valley of the Sun, and as a portion of *Predestined Love* published by Simon & Schuster Pocket Books in 1988. In *Reinventing Yourself*, the Critical 13 has been expanded to 15 factors, and many additional dialogues have been added.

CONTENTS

Chapter One
THE CRITICAL 15

How to reinvent yourself is easy.

All you have to do is decide what you want, and discover what is keeping you from having it. Then rise above the effects of the traps that are blocking you, and approach your goals in a realistic way. Easier said than done? Of course, but you can reinvent yourself if you are sincere in your quest and willing to proceed one step at a time.

To begin, if your life is not working the way you want it to work, you need to examine the nature of your traps. More often than not, there is no difference between yourself and the trap. This being the case, you are not trapped. *Reinventing Yourself* begins by addressing the Critical 15 traps from a metaphysical/human-potential perspective.

Having already written several books on the subject of reincarnation and karma, I will not attempt to substantiate their validity in this volume. Chapter seventeen, however, offers a brief explanation, and if you don't have an understanding of the subject, you may want to read this chapter first. Many of your problems are caused by beliefs stemming from past lives as well as present-life experiences.

Critical to reinventing yourself is the ability to choose wisely between realistic and unrealistic behavior—what we call reason. This relates to most of the Critical 15 traps. If you were to go into psychotherapy, the doctor would work to get you to be more responsible and realistic about your decisions, and to show you the value in making immediate sacrifices for the sake of long-term satisfaction.

Therapists usually work from the premise that you have problems because you are unable to fulfill your essential needs. We all have the same needs but we differ in our ability to fulfill them. The severity of your symptoms is a direct reflection of your inability to fulfill those needs. But whatever your symptoms, they will disappear when your needs are aligned with reality and successfully fulfilled.

The practice of psychiatry is concerned with two basic psychological needs: **1. The need to love and be loved.** You need at least one person in your life to love and who loves you in return. Without this essential person, you will be unable to fulfill your basic needs.

2. The need to feel worthwhile to yourself and others. To maintain high self-esteem you must maintain a satisfactory standard of behavior and correct yourself when you are wrong. If your behavior is below your standard and you don't correct it, you will suffer as a result. You must fulfill your needs in a way that does not deprive others of the ability to fulfill their needs.

When you decide what behaviors are not serving you, be aware that an immediate change in behavior will lead to a change in attitude. You don't have to change how you feel about something to affect it, if you are willing to change what you are doing. Exerting the self-discipline to make immediate changes in your behavior will lead to a change in attitude. *Actions influence attitude.* An improved attitude will lead to fulfilling your needs and further improved behavior, which will increase your self-esteem.

The Critical 15

For 15 years I've taught a five-day seminar called the **Professional Past-Life Therapy Training.** The participants come from all over the world to learn hypnosis, regression and counseling techniques. Some incorporate the awareness into their existing careers, while others use it to establish a hypnosis/counseling practice. A few of those in attendance are practicing psychologists and psychiatrists. Many are wholistic practitioners, Reiki, Shiatsu or Reflexology therapists who want to expand their practices to be of further service to their clients. Others plan to incorporate the seminar awareness into careers as human-potential trainers.

This professional training covers many areas of expertise, yet basic to all the awareness is what I call the *Critical 15*—the foundation of *Reinventing Yourself.* When someone explains his problem to a counselor or stands up in a seminar room to share his pain, *the cause of his turmoil will always be one or more of these 15 traps.* So, the counselor/therapist/trainer must learn to listen for these factors in the verbal exchange with his subject. Usually one or more of the 15 factors will quickly become obvious. The therapist then begins verbal "processing" by asking the right questions; the subject's answers indicate the next step in the processing. Once the therapist understands the problem, he may use "Back To The Cause" hypnotic regression techniques where there appears to be no known cause.

No counselor, therapist, minister or friend playing the part of a counselor, should ever advise another person what to do. Instead, verbally guide the individual through his conflict and into the light of awareness. Let a troubled person discover his own answers.

The Critical 15

- **Beliefs**
- **Assumed Limitations & Faulty Assumptions**
- **Blaming & Victims**
- **Negative Payoffs**
- **Masks Or Acts**
- **Incompatible Goals & Values**
- **Resistance To "What Is"**
- **Mirroring**
- **Fear**
- **The Need To Be Right**
- **Expectations**
- **Clarity Of Intent**
- **Lack Of Aliveness Or Motivation**
- **Lack Of Self-Discipline**
- **Misplaced Passion**

Whatever a therapist can do, you can do for yourself, if you're willing to ask the right questions and explore your own past. The explanations and case histories offered in this book are to use as a basis for self-processing. If your problem relates to a past life, you can choose to work with a profes-sional hypnotist, regress yourself, or use prerecorded hyp-notic regression tapes to find the cause of your present effects.

After explaining each of the Critical 15 traps, I will provide the general action required to rise above the nega-tivity, and then I'll demonstrate the factor in action, using seminar dialogues tape recorded in my *Bushido, Master of Life* and *Satori* seminars. The seminars are conducted in hotel ballrooms, with 100 to 300 people in attendance. Seminar participants may ask for the microphone and inter-act with me if they desire, but they are never forced or asked individually to share.

Out of the context of a seminar or counseling session, the encounters often appear cold and unfeeling to a reader. In reality, they are a form of "hard love," for the therapist/trainer has one goal in mind—to create the space for the individual to help himself, by finding his own truths. The trainer/participant association is a modern-day version of the Zen Master/student association. The seminar training (as in Zen) is a process of seeking to find in self, the path to liberation.

Zen is neither a religion nor a philosophy, but a way of liberation. It is a game of discovering who you are beneath your programming. The Zen Master often used a stick to hit a student who wasn't "getting it." In the seminars, I pur-posely use attitudes and words as my stick. One participant might react best to shock, another to gentle support, another to teasing, et cetera. My goal is to guide the participant to become aware of his own self-defeating attitudes and behav-ior, and to jolt him out of his intellectual ruts, passé notions, and convictions that are restricting his life. To be effective, I must be willing to incur his dislike. As in Zen, the participant is encouraged to leap into the unknown and find his truth within. His inner, True Self is found when the false, fearful self is renounced.

(NOTE: Many of the dialogues in this book have been condensed to more quickly make the point.)

 *"I don't love him, but no one else is interested in me—I have no choice."*

Chapter Two
BELIEFS

A belief is something you don't know. A negative belief is obviously based in fear, but positive beliefs can also be based on fear. Look at some common beliefs that appear to be positive yet are fear-based: You believe your country is the greatest in the world; you believe in the goodness of God; that your mate is faithful; in the loyalty of your friends, in job security. To believe otherwise is fearful. You may even believe UFOs are abducting people, or that the Harmonic Convergence was valid. But you don't know any of these things for sure. You may even be willing to stake your life on what you believe, but your faith doesn't make the belief valid.

You are served by many of your positive beliefs, but it is important to realize which of them are based on fear. Beliefs generate your thoughts and emotions which create all your experiences. These beliefs are the result of two things: Your present-life programming resulting from experiences and influences, such as parents, church, and society, and past-life programming resulting in fear-based beliefs that generate self-defeating blocks to the attainment of happiness and success.

Beliefs are not buried deep in the subconscious mind. They are part of our conscious awareness, they just go unexamined because they've been accepted as *facts*. But there are few facts in life. What we accept as reality is primarily constructed of beliefs about the way things are and ideas about how they should be.

Sure, it's easy to recognize your surface beliefs about such things as religion and politics, but I'm talking about core beliefs—who and what you are and how that relates to your success, weight, health, relationships or lack of relationships, career, and everything else central to your existence.

As examples: You believe you can only reach a certain level of success, so that's as successful as you are. You believe your body is fat, so you are. If you change your belief, your subconscious programming changes and your body weight will align with the new programming. Hypnosis, subliminal and sleep programming tapes, which are so popular today, do only one thing: they change old beliefs by programming the subconscious mind with new beliefs.

Self-processing of resentments related to your beliefs can also be valuable. A Universal law says *you cannot become what you resent.* This law is absolute because *you always live up to your self-image.* As an example, let's say you are overweight and when you see someone with a beautiful body, you make a snide comment such as, "All beauty and no brains." In so doing, you doom yourself to being overweight because if people with beautiful bodies have no brains, you will never allow yourself to have a beautiful body. You certainly don't want to be brainless.

As another example, let's say you are actively seeking financial success, but at a stoplight, when you pull up beside a Rolls-Royce, you look over and think, "Rich people are such snobs." Now you are assuring that you will never be rich. You wouldn't allow yourself to have the self-image of a snob.

Action Required

Your disharmonious beliefs are like walls surrounding you and restricting your life. If you want to tear down the walls, first you must recognize they exist, and that you are not free. You can't change what you don't recognize. Once you are aware of the undesirable beliefs, you can begin the process of reinvention by taking the following steps:

1. Examine the belief in relationship to reality. The belief needs to be tested against *"what is."*

2. If you don't know the source of the belief, it will probably serve you to find it with regressive hypnosis.

3. Begin altered-state reprogramming using self-hypnosis or prerecorded tapes.

4. If you know the belief isn't logical as it relates to your current life, and you know the cause, start forgiving yourself and anyone else involved in the experience that created the belief. Include the following mantra as part of your daily meditation or programming sessions:

"I know the cause of this situation and I now release the effect. I forgive myself and everyone else involved, and in so doing I release the effect and liberate myself." Chant it over and over in the altered state as you visualize yourself free of the effect.

The following dialogues will help you to better understand belief as a programming factor.

Adelle:
Seminar Dialogue

Adelle, a dark-haired beauty in her early thirties, raised her hand to request a microphone. "It isn't logical, but I realized in the group belief process that my belief about marriage is, 'All the good men are already taken, so don't bother.'"

"What is your experience in regard to the belief?" I asked.

"Well, I guess I think this. But actually I have lots of dates, and many of the men are great. However, I never let them get very serious." She flashed an amused grin.

"Would you like to get married if you found the right man?"

"Yes, consciously I would. But you've got me concerned about my subconscious programming." She shrugged matter-of-factly. "I'd hate to be fooling myself for the next twenty years."

Seminar participants are taught a technique for instant hypnosis. This allows me to quickly regress individuals during the processing sessions. Adelle wanted to explore the cause of her belief, so I directed the induction process and told her, "You may go back to an earlier time in your present life, or you may return to an event that transpired in a previous incarnation. On the count of three, you'll experience vivid impressions relating to the cause of your belief about men and marriage. One, two, three."

She was silent for a moment before her eyes started to move rapidly beneath her closed eyelids. When she spoke, her voice was soft and low. "There's a woman...she's crying."

"Are you the woman?" I asked.

"I think so. She's about to be married but she isn't very happy about it."

"I want you to attain a complete understanding of the situation. You have the power and ability to do this. Move forward in time if necessary. When you have the awareness, speak up and share it with me."

Adelle was silent, and she breathed deeply. "My father says I should be married. My sisters are all married, my friends are married. He's afraid I'm going to be an old maid, so I am marrying Reece." She hesitated, and for a moment I thought she was going to burst into tears. "I don't love him, but no one else is interested in me—I have no choice."

After exploring additional details of this lifetime, I directed Adelle to let go of the past-life impressions and ascend into the all-knowing superconscious or Higher-Self portion of mind. "All right, Adelle, I want you to talk to me about how this relates to your present life."

"Obviously, my belief has been programmed by a fear of repeating a painful past-life experience. It will block me until I confront it. If I'm open to loving and being loved, I can rise above this old programming."

Daryl:
Seminar Dialogue

"Beliefs About Old Pain" is one of four group belief processes in my Satori Seminar. In the first portion of these sessions, I ask the hypnotized participants to complete incomplete sentences. The altered state makes it easier to get your conscious mind out of the way, allowing awareness to be drawn from the subconscious. "Don't think about it, just let the words flow into your mind and complete the sentence," I tell them. "This can expose beliefs you didn't even know you had."

During the second portion of the process the participants choose one belief about old pain to explore in greater depth. I tell them, "You're going to go back in time to the cause of this belief. You may go back to an earlier time in your present life or you may return to an event that transpired in a previous incarnation." I then direct a regression and the session ends with further processing and forgiveness.

Usually the new awareness gleaned in the old-pain process causes some of the participants to cry. When I've awakened the group, I say, "If anyone needs a tissue, put up your hand and the support team will bring it to you."

Daryl was about 40, conservatively dressed, with shoulder-length brown hair. She was sitting on the aisle in the third row, and I noticed her take several tissues from the box. Blotting her eyes with one hand, she made notes on a yellow legal pad with the other. When I asked if anyone had any questions or comments, she was among the first to raise her hand.

Dabbing the tissue to the corner of her eye, she stood up, took the microphone and said, "When you said, 'If I were to look back on my life and say anyone abused me, it would have to be...'" She took a deep breath and looked down at the floor. Then she looked at me and said, "I completed it by saying, 'My uncle Paul.'"

"Yes?" I said.

"Well, that's off the wall. My uncle Paul never abused me.

I mean, if he did I'd certainly remember it, wouldn't I?"

"Not necessarily," I said. "Your mind is capable of blocking painful memories, but they remain under the surface, festering like an infected wound, poisoning you."

"I didn't explore the potential of Uncle Paul's abuse in the regression portion of the session, because I wanted to find out about the cause of my painful relationship with my ex-husband," Daryl said.

Following an intuitive feeling, I said, "Are you willing to share what you found out about your husband?"

Daryl nodded, dabbed her eye and said, "My basic belief about men is, all they want is sex. And when you said to complete the sentence that started, 'When I think about old lovers and ex-mates, I have to admit that ...' " Daryl sniffled. "I finished it, 'I have to admit that all any of them ever wanted from me was sex.' "

"And do you still believe that?"

"Yes, but I think it's my karma. In the regression, I saw myself as a moneylender, an ugly man, in England I think. Probably the eighteen-hundreds. I loaned money to women in exchange for sexual favors. Many were desperate, with husbands out of work and children to feed."

"Would you like to regress back and explore the abuse by Uncle Paul?"

Daryl nodded. I had her step out into the aisle. A support team member stood behind her, holding the microphone, while I used the conditioned-response technique to put her into a deep hypnotic sleep and direct her back into the past. "If there was ever a time your Uncle Paul abused you, you are to return to that time as an observer, without pain and without emotion, on the count of three. One, two, three."

Daryl swayed, groaned, and a deep frown furrowed her forehead.

"Speak up and tell me what you see and what you are doing," I said.

She tried to talk and seemed to choke on the words. Then she said, "Uncle Paul makes me put his thing in my mouth. I hate it. HATE IT! It tastes bad and he smells." Her voice was that of a young girl.

"How old are you, Daryl?"

"Six."

"How often does Uncle Paul make you do this?"

"Every time Mama has him babysit me, which is a lot."

"How old is Uncle Paul?"

She didn't respond for a moment, then said, "Seventeen, I think."

I directed Daryl to let go of the situation, to ascend up into her Higher Self, and we called in her spirit guide. "You have now transcended levels of mind, and if you are willing to trust your thoughts, feelings and visualizations, you have complete knowledge of your totality at your mental finger-tips. Do you accept this?" Daryl nodded. "If you have experienced many men who seemed to want you for sex, it was a karmic balance you needed to experience. Do you understand this?"

"Yes."

"You've felt that you were the victim of men who wanted you for sex, but from a karmic perspective there are no victims. You and you alone are responsible for everything that has ever happened to you. But until you recognize your role of victim, you can't release it and realize that you were never a victim at all. Everyone in your past was exactly what you needed them to be in order for you to learn and grow."

"To balance what I did to the women back in England?"

"Possibly. There may be more to it, but none of it matters if you're ready to forgive yourself, and forgive your ex-lovers, ex-husband, Uncle Paul, and everyone else who you feel has abused you."

Daryl didn't respond.

"Wisdom erases karma, Daryl. You can release yourself from this chain of cause and effect if you can forgive yourself and everyone else involved."

"I'm going to have to think about it."

"All right, on the count of five you will open your eyes and be wide awake, fully alert, thinking and acting with calm self-assurance. You'll remember everything you just experienced and be at peace with yourself, the world and everyone in it."

When she was awake and holding the microphone, Daryl said, "I wanted to say, 'Yes, I forgive myself and everyone else,' but that wasn't what I felt in here." She touched her stomach. "It wouldn't do any good to say it and not mean it, would it?"

I shook my head.

"If I can let go of the past, do you think I can find a relationship ... a good relationship?"

"Yes."

"I've never had a good relationship. Thank you," she said, handing the microphone back to the support team member and sitting down.

(NOTE: During the second day of the seminar, Daryl made another personal breakthrough that demonstrated the power of self-forgiveness. At this time she tearfully forgave

herself and all the men in her past.)

An Overview

Both Adelle's and Daryl's situations stemmed from beliefs that are, at the same time, other Critical 15 traps: Adelle's belief that all the good men are taken was a "faulty assumption." Daryl's belief that men only wanted her for sex also falls under "blaming and victims." There were "negative payoffs" for both women in maintaining the status quo. Adelle's position allowed her to avoid the pain she subconsciously associated with relationships. Daryl's position allowed her to balance her karma. And "fear" was ultimately responsible for both situations.

Graham:
Seminar Dialogue

"Would you please read the third sentence you asked us to complete in that process?" Graham asked. He was in his thirties, wore circular glasses, had a businessman's haircut and was dressed in a tweed sport coat with leather elbow pads.

The session we'd just completed was the Career/Success Belief Process. I looked at my notebook and read the sentence. "Someone said that being responsible and playing it safe is more important than loving what you do. I think the person who said that is ..."

Graham said, "That's it. I finished it, 'is absolutely right.'"

"And ..." I raised my hands gesturing him to go on.

"That's not what I should have said. I think it's really important to love what you do."

"Maybe you're 'shoulding' on yourself, Graham. Do you

love what you do?''

"No, not now, but I'm moving toward it. I'm planning for it. Someday, I'm sure I'll be doing what I really enjoy, but I keep putting it off."

"Did you explore the cause of this belief in the regression portion of the process?"

"No, something else that proved valuable, but it has nothing to do with this. Would you regress me to find out why I answered that way?"

Three minutes later, Graham was in deep hypnosis. "It's time for you to explore the idea of doing what you love to do," I said. "If there is any fear in this concept, I want you to move back in time to the cause of the fear." When his eyes began to flutter beneath his eyelids, I asked, "What do you see and what are you doing?"

"I'm writing at a desk." He chuckled. "Man, am I dressed funny."

"What are you writing?"

"My weekly editorial. I'm the editor of the paper and ..." He hesitated. "It's a time of great unrest. The people are divided. Many people support what I write, but it is also hated by many others."

"All right, let's move forward in time until something important happens as the result of your writing. On the count of three you'll be there, one, two, three."

"Oh-h-h-h, my God. FOOLS, BLOODY FOOLS." Graham began to cry.

"All right, let go of this and let's move on up into your all-knowing Higher Self. Let go now, and ascend, ascend, ascend." When the instructions were complete and Graham was calm once more, I asked him to explain what happened.

27

"They killed my wife, burned down the newspaper office and then killed me."

"Do you understand that what happened in the past does not relate to enjoying your work in the present, Graham?"

"Yes."

"No one will murder you for doing what you love today."

When the session was over I explained that Graham was experiencing "false fear karma." This is a matter of a traumatic past-life incident generating a fear that is not valid in the context of the current life. It is one of the easiest kinds of karma to resolve. Often, knowing the cause is enough to free the individual of the effect.

I suggested that Graham incorporate a new mantra into his meditations or programming sessions: "I understand the cause of my past anxiety over loving what I do, and I release myself from the effect, forgiving myself and everyone else involved. And I now establish a successful career doing what I really enjoy."

* * * * *

Although I'll categorize the 14 traps that follow by different titles, they are all actually beliefs rooted in self-deception and fear. *Delusionary beliefs* are the basic problem in everyone's life. But by breaking various aspects of belief down into a system of 15 easily identifiable categories, it is easier to learn and incorporate into your life.

If you accept reincarnation and karma, you probably wonder why you are here on the earth and what you are supposed to be doing with the time you have. Wonder no more. *Your earthly purpose is to cast away your delusions.*

For nearly twenty years, I've been telling people in seminars that they are here to learn to let go of fear and to express unconditional love. Your fear-based emotions are delusions: prejudice, anger, selfishness, jealousy, hate, repression, envy, greed, possessiveness, guilt, egotism, and all the other negative emotions are responses to past programming. These undesirable, unnecessary fears keep you earthbound on the endless wheel of reincarnation. Even the expression of unconditional love is a matter of casting away fearful delusions, for unconditional love is the acceptance of other people as they are, without judgment, expectations or blame.

Beneath your fearful programming, you are an enlightened soul. So, the way to liberate yourself is to cast away your delusions, so you can more fully realize what you already are.

Chapter Three

ASSUMED LIMITATIONS
& FAULTY ASSUMPTIONS

These factors are active in our lives to some degree. Here are some examples: "I'm a $25,000 a year commissioned sales rep, but I'm not capable of being a $75,000 a year man." "If I'm direct and honest in my communications, I'll probably lose all my friends." "I'd really love to have a good relationship, but it isn't possible being married to Fred."

Usually, assumed limitations and faulty assumptions are directly related to your self-image and the size of your vision. Until you become aware of your mental limitations, it is unlikely you'll do anything to rise above them.

Action Required

Realize that the limitations and assumptions are self-imposed beliefs. They are not real. The next step to rising above the effects of restrictive thinking is to become clear on your intent. Exactly what do you want, why do you want it, and what are you willing to do to get it?

Mark:
Seminar Dialogue

"I don't think it is a faulty assumption to realistically appraise your limitations," Mark said, challenge in his voice. He was in his late thirties, wore his hair longer than usual, and dressed casually.

"Apply this to your life, Mark. What are you talking about?" I asked, leaving the stage to move closer to him.

"I'd like to marry a beautiful woman, but I'm neither handsome nor successful enough to attract one."

"What does love have to do with you being handsome or successful?" I asked.

"I didn't say anything about love," he snapped.

"Oh, you just want to marry her as a showpiece?"

"Well, ah, no. It's just that it would make me feel good if she were beautiful."

"What if she is a stark-raving, beautiful bitch, instead?"

He shrugged his shoulders and tilted his head to one side, in reply.

"What's really going on with you, Mark? This has nothing to do with beautiful women."

"I don't know what you mean."

"Yes, you do. Who would be impressed by your beautiful wife?"

Mark's eyes narrowed and he gave me a hard, cynical smile. "Everybody!"

"Everybody, huh? What would they think about you because you had a beautiful wife?"

He hesitated momentarily, then blurted, "That I must

really be something special to get her!"

"That's a faulty assumption, Mark. You're attempting to bolster your self-image externally, which will never work. We all have a basic psychological need to feel worthwhile to ourselves and others. But self-image results from what we do in life, not from what we have. Also—and this is critical to your self-image—you must maintain a satisfactory standard of behavior and correct yourself when you're wrong. When your conduct is below your standard and you don't correct it, your self-image will suffer. When you do things that make you feel good about yourself, your self-image is enhanced."

"Well, that's a lot easier said than done," Mark responded impatiently.

"Feeling more worthy begins with examining your behavior. Wise choices between realistic and unrealistic behavior is simply what we call reason. Tell me what you do that makes you feel good about yourself."

He hesitated, looked at the floor, crossing and uncrossing his arms. "Ah, well, nothing now, but I'd like to go to night school and learn about computers so I can get a better job. But I haven't had the time."

"You've just been 'way too busy,' huh?" I said in a sympathetic tone.

"Yes." He realized I was mocking him and scowled. "Well, maybe the reason I'm not all that responsible is karma?"

"Everything is karma, so I'm sure it is. But wisdom erases karma, Mark. If you were regularly visiting one of the new breed of psychotherapists, he would try to get you to be more responsible and realistic about making immediate sacrifices to attain long-term satisfaction."

"I can't afford therapy," he said.

"You don't need therapy to make a decision to be self-responsible."

He didn't respond.

"If I were you, Mark, I'd consider working on my self-image. And instead of looking for a beautiful woman, look for the *right* woman—someone you can love and who will love you. If you find her, she'll be beautiful to you no matter what she looks like."

Mark nodded.

"Decide what you really want and why you want it. You need to want it for the right reasons or it won't work when you get it."

"Thank you," he said, sitting down.

"Stay tuned for everything else we'll be discussing in this seminar, Mark. Many of the other concepts will also relate to your situation."

Catherine:
Seminar Dialogue

"One of the best ways to increase self-esteem is to value *being* more than *belonging*," I said to the group. "This means to value what is right and true for you more than what other people think. It can take courage, but courage is important to high self-esteem. Courageous people are a minority, as are those with high self-esteem. But those with high self-esteem have superior relationships and are more independent and direct in their communications. They express who they are and what they believe, without being concerned about what other people think. This is often intimidating to those whose self-esteem restricts them to thinking and living conventionally."

Catherine raised her hand and was given a microphone. A dark, exotic-looking woman in her late twenties or early thirties, she was wearing a sport coat, white blouse with a bolo tie, and silk pants. "I disagree with you. More often than not it is self-destructive to express who you *really* are and what you *really* believe."

"I contend that's a faulty assumption," I said. "But why don't you give me an example to change my mind?"

"All right. I'm a fashion model and I work for overly sensitive fashion designers. If I were to tell them what I *really* think of their clothes, they'd never hire me again."

"I agree. You're hired to model the clothes, not critique them. Refraining from expressing your opinion in a situation like that doesn't cause you to experience repression and stress, does it?"

"No, it's just an example from my life."

"Give me an example of repressing who you are that does cause you stress."

Catherine looked out the ballroom windows overlooking a Manhattan street two floors below. "My boyfriend. My lover. He frustrates me, and when I express my frustrations, he blows up."

"What is right and true for you that causes him to blow up?"

"My daily need for a little quiet time alone. My desire to become an actress as well as a model. My love of classical music." Lowering the microphone, Catherine folded her arms and waited for me to respond.

"So you think it's better to wear a mask and be who your

boyfriend wants you to be, than to be who you really are?"

"My life is more peaceful."

"Are you more peaceful? Repressing who you are usually creates problems: stress, anxiety, resentment, nervousness, any of which can manifest in physical problems."

"I hate fighting."

"How long do you think you can repress who you are? A year? Two years? Five years?"

"Certainly not five years."

"Do you think your boyfriend is going to change?"

Catherine laughed. "No."

"Then your relationship is terminal. You've given it less than five years."

She stared at me. I continued. "Going back to where this exchange began, I contend it is self-destructive not to express what is right and true for you. If much of your relationship is based on repression, your needs are not being fulfilled and problems will eventually result. You'll have to decide for yourself how you'll be better served in the long run."

(NOTE: The above dialogue went quickly from a "faulty assumption" to another Critical 15 factor, "masks or acts." As a counselor, trainer or a friend helping a friend, you have to decide which route to follow, drawing awareness of both factors. At the same time you know that you are always dealing with "fear," and the cause will be rooted in "beliefs." In a situation like Catherine's, I rarely use hypnotic regression. Once she had the awareness attained in the dialogue, she would choose to act or to wait until she is so frustrated she has to act. The result will be the same either way, but by acting earlier she might save herself years of

frustration and lost career opportunities.)

Kenneth:
Seminar Dialogue

"Coming from a dysfunctional family, you always have several strikes against you," Kenneth said. He was in his early forties, thin, conservatively dressed, and he seemed nervous about speaking into the microphone.

"That's true," I said.

"You agree?" he said, surprised.

"If you want to assume that limitation or faulty assumption, then, yes, it's true for you."

"I don't want it to be true for me, but it's a fact."

"No. I know many people who have come from dysfunctional families who are quite happy and successful. It isn't true for them."

"But John Bradshaw says ..."

"I don't care what anyone says. You came into this life to experience the karma of a dysfunctional family. It was your choice. Once you recognize the situation for what it is, you can use the awareness to release the effect."

"Just like that?" Kenneth's left eye was twitching.

"Maybe. Tell me about the strikes against you resulting from your dysfunctional family."

He shuffled back and forth from one foot to the other. "Well, I've never been able to sustain a relationship for very long. I've had my own problems with drugs. There's an anger in here." He pointed to his stomach.

"And you blame your family?"

"Who else would I blame? I know I'm supposed to forgive them, but I haven't been able to do that."

"What about forgiving yourself?"

He shook his head. "I didn't do anything to them."

"Want to find out?"

"What? If I did anything to them?"

After some explanation, Kenneth agreed to be regressed to the cause of his being born into a dysfunctional family in this life. I had to relax him three times and stress over and over, "Trust the impressions that flow into your mind in response to my questions." When his physical body was relaxed and his eyes began moving rapidly beneath his eyelids, I guided him back to the cause. "What do you perceive, what are you doing?"

He laughed, a cold, sadistic laugh. "I'm tossin' leftover grub into the hold. An' when they scurry for it, we throw stuff at 'em."

"Why are the people scurrying for the food?"

"Prisoners. We're transportin' them to their new home." He laughed again.

"On a ship?"

"Yeah."

"And they're hungry?"

"Starvin', more likely."

"And you use them for targets ... for sport?"

"They're nothin' but cruisers and cracks."

"What are cruisers and cracks?"

Kenneth laughed, shook his head and said, "No-goods and whores."

"And you serve on a ship that transports them from ..."

"Of course. Back and forth, back and forth."

"And you enjoy seeing these people suffer?" I asked.

"They ain't people, I told ya."

I instructed Kenneth to remember everything he was perceiving, but to ascend up into the higher realms of his mind. When he had attained a Higher-Self level of awareness, I said, "In directing you to return to the cause, you perceived a life as a seaman in which you were very cruel to prisoners. How does that incarnation relate to you being born into a dysfunctional family?"

"I chose to be born to unloving, dominating parents so I could experience firsthand the effect of my actions in that English lifetime. Even my two brothers and one sister in this life were people I mistreated in that life, not in the hold of the ship, but years later when I was a prison guard."

"So maybe it's a faulty assumption to blame your current family for your problems."

"I need to learn to be loving."

"How can you rise above the problems in your life?"

"Forgiveness. Forgiving myself, and forgiving my family. I have to give love to receive love. I think I've always been waiting for other people to love me first."

Robin:
Seminar Dialogue

"All the good men are taken, just like Adelle said. They really are. I don't expect you to believe that, but it's true," Robin said, her big blue eyes looking directly into mine. Slender and vivacious, she was probably in her late twenties, and dressed in jeans and a Harvard sweatshirt.

"All of them are taken?" I said.

"What's left are married men who mess around, nerds, losers, dopers, plug uglies and a drifty or two or twenty."

"A drifty?" I said.

"The stupidly inattentive."

I nodded. "How many good ones were there?"

"Not many."

"How many?"

"I've only known two. Both were boyfriends. Both left me for other women."

"So there were only two good men in the country, and now other women have them?"

"You're playing with my head."

"*You're* playing with your head. You know there are plenty of good men, but you're not open to them."

"You can't imagine how open I would be to the right man. Seriously, I just don't meet any."

"Well, let's say you were to meet Mr. Right. What would this mean to your lifestyle? A lot of things would change, wouldn't they?"

"Sure. I'd start having regular male sex, for one thing."

"The way you said that sounds like you're having irregular, unmale sex?"

"I have sex with women. In bed I orient to both men and women."

"Would you want to continue having sex with women after meeting Mr. Right?"

"Sure, occasionally. But that wouldn't affect him."

"Some men would have a problem with it."

"Then he wouldn't be Mr. Right, would he?"

"What else would change when Mr. Right moves in with you?"

"Who said anything about him moving in with me? Maybe later, you know. But I'm not in any hurry to start washing a man's clothes, or cooking his meals, or putting down the toilet seat every time I want to use it."

"Oh-h-h-h-h-h-h-h-h-h-h," sounded from the audience.

"Isn't it interesting, Robin, that the only changes you've mentioned so far are negative changes?"

She shrugged. "Another is football and basketball on TV. No way, Jose."

"Robin, you still haven't mentioned anything positive."

"Yes, I did. Sex with a man."

"What else?"

"Maybe having kids someday."

"You can get a kid at the sperm bank. Name some other positive aspects of meeting Mr. Right."

Robin hesitated, so I said, "Tell me why your two boyfriends left you for other women."

Slowly drawing one hand up to her hip, she said, "They didn't feel I was very loving to them. And one of them found out I was also sleeping with my girlfriend."

I waited. She didn't say any more, so I said, "Maybe you need to make it all right with yourself to be a lesbian?"

Robin looked at me, shocked. Then her eyes started to mist, and a moment later she burst into tears. "I made it all right with myself to be whatever I wanted to be a long time ago. I just can't make it all right with my family. My mother and father would be crushed to find out their daughter is bisexual."

"You can't live for your family."

"My mother calls three times a week wanting to know if I've met any 'interesting' men. You have no idea what it's like. Thank God they live in another city."

"Living a lie takes a lot of energy."

"It's not a lie. I just don't want to hurt my folks. Plus, if

41

the real Mr. Right came along, I'd go for him." She sighed deeply. "Fat chance, huh?"

"Not if you're ready to give and receive love from a man. A relationship has to work inside and outside the bedroom. There are probably plenty of men who wouldn't mind their wife sleeping with a woman, but it does reduce your chances of finding Mr. Right. If you were willing to share the woman with your husband, you could probably count on a much higher percentage of men who would go for it. But you'll have to be clear on your intent and direct and honest in your communications."

 *"My husband ran off with my best friend, and you're telling me not to blame?"*

Chapter Four
BLAMING & VICTIMS

It is easier to be a victim and blame others for your circumstances than it is to take responsibility for your life. From a metaphysical perspective, blame is incompatible with reincarnation and karma. We are here on earth to learn, and we set up the circumstances as tests to judge our level of awareness. Since you assigned yourself your lessons, there is no one but yourself to blame for anything you've ever experienced.

So, think about all the people who have victimized you: your mate who divorced you, your friend who betrayed you, your business partner who ripped you off. You can't blame them. They supplied the opportunities you needed to experience. Thank them. Release them.

From a human-potential perspective, blame is self-pity. Relate this to your life and you'll realize how true it is. Plus, self-pity is negative programming of your subconscious mind, so it is doubly destructive.

Action Required

Realize the futility of blame. You are the only one harmed by the illusion. The acceptance of self-actualized metaphysical philosophy will transform the way you experience the negativity.

Gregory:
Seminar Dialogue

"Everything is changing, speeding up, becoming more chaotic. It's almost impossible to plan for the future. I'm spread so thin I don't have enough time to do what I need to do," Gregory said. He was in his late forties, a distinguished-looking man in a blue blazer, white shirt and tan pants.

"Are you a victim of chaos, Gregory?"

"I'm serious," he said, scowling. "It used to be different, and it's driving me crazy. All the rules seem to have changed."

"Living with chaos is a metaphor for our time, and it often requires a kinetic lifestyle. Instead of fighting chaos, why not invent new organizing principles with plenty of open ends—a temporary order for as long as you need it. This can allow you to maneuver, think and make decisions without driving yourself crazy. Focus on the present with your eye on the future."

"Easier said than done. I own my own business and the business climate has become so unpredictable." Gregory said.

"You can always choose not to play. Sell out and move to Montana where you can live a simple life."

"I couldn't leave Los Angeles."

"Then consider embracing chaos as the new order. Stop

resisting it. Everything is changing—the familiar order is giving way to new orders we don't yet fully understand. Accept that the world is discontinuous and unpredictable, and use your energy to look for the new opportunities that always come out of chaos."

Gregory nodded, thoughtfully.

I continued. "In regard to your being spread so thin in this chaotic world. Who's at fault?"

"A lot of people make demands on me. My company, my wife and family, friends, organizations. It's overwhelming."

"So you blame them rather than yourself?"

"I can't turn my back on them."

"Yes, you can, but first you have to accept that you aren't a victim of their demands. You are experiencing exactly what you set yourself up to experience."

He shook his head. "You mean karma?"

"Tell me how you'd like it to be, Gregory. A typical day in your life."

Without hesitation, he said, "I'd like to go to work for eight hours, come home, relax and watch the six P.M. news, have dinner with my wife and kids and spend the evening reading a good book."

"Your wish is granted. Do it."

Gregory laughed. Then he said, "I often have to work overtime."

"Not if you delegate responsibility. Not if you hire some extra help."

"It's not quite that easy." He paused. "Friends call all evening."

"Get an answering machine and return all the calls at one time—maybe Saturday afternoon."

"I do a lot of work with social organizations."

"Stop doing it. It's your life, not theirs."

"Come on. You're advocating lack of responsibility."

"I'm advocating that you be responsible to yourself first. It's your life. You have to control it. Ask your mate, children, parents, in-laws, employees, friends, and the social organizations what they feel your priorities should be and I'm sure everyone will give you a different answer. But no one else can relate to your position and know what is best for you. It's your value judgment as to what you will do with your time and in what order you choose to accomplish your tasks. It is also your right to choose whether or not to accept any responsibility for other people's needs."

When Gregory didn't respond, I continued. "The old eighty/twenty plan says you get eighty percent of your results from twenty percent of your efforts. Simplify, and focus on the twenty percent of your efforts that pay the best dividends at work and at home. It's also easier to maneuver the twenty percent, allowing you to quickly respond to a chaotic environment."

Gregory nodded again and sat down.

Earle & Sarah:
Seminar Dialogue

"I got into an affair because my relationship at home was boring. I still love my wife and kids, but it's turned into a mess and my wife is talking about a divorce." Earle was a beefy man who appeared to work out regularly. I guessed him to be in his middle thirties. He was dressed in jeans and a turtleneck.

"Whose fault was it that the relationship was boring?" I

asked.

"My wife is a stick-in-the-mud. She doesn't like to do anything." Earle turned and looked at the woman sitting beside him.

"Is this your wife?" I nodded at the woman. Her name tag read SARAH.

Earle nodded. Sarah said, "Yes."

"What is your idea of fun, of doing something?" I asked Earle.

"Going out to clubs. Movies. You know."

"Didn't you know that Sarah didn't enjoy these things before you got married?"

"She used to, but she changed after we had kids. She refuses to get a babysitter, so we can't go any place we can't take the kids."

Sarah said softly, "I'm afraid something will happen to them if we leave them."

"So you punished Sarah by having an affair?"

"It wasn't like that. I did meet Julie at a nightclub, but the affair just happened. It wasn't to punish Sarah."

"How did Sarah find out about it?"

"I told her. I felt guilty."

"But you didn't stop the affair?"

"I couldn't."

"Poor Earle," I said.

"Give me a break," he replied, scowling. "I came here thinking you could help us find out why our life is such a mess. Maybe it relates to a past life."

"Maybe. But what's important is, what do you want to happen now?"

"I wish I could just have my mind erased," he said sadly.

"What would you erase?"

"Julie. Then I could be with my wife and kids and not be torn like I am."

"Did you ever consider why Sarah was so fearful of leaving the children at home?"

Earle shrugged. Sarah shook her head.

I asked Sarah if she would like to explore the fear. She agreed and a few minutes later was deep in an altered state of consciousness. I directed her back to the cause of her fear. As she stepped out of the subjective tunnel into the past, she took a deep breath and screamed, "Oh my, God!" When she wouldn't calm down, I removed her from the past and directed her to ascend up into Higher Self. From this perspective she was able to calmly explain what had happened.

"I was working with my husband in the fields. I don't think it was Earle in another incarnation, he felt more like my father in this life. The babies were asleep in the cabin. The cabin caught fire and by the time we noticed and made our way back home, it was too late," she said, sniffling. "They'd breathed in too much smoke. Our daughter died. Our son lived, but his lungs were so weak he died of pneumonia the following winter."

"And this terrible experience created a fear that has carried over into this life," I said. "But what happened in the past doesn't relate to the present. It's a false fear. If you leave your children with a good babysitter, they'll be safe. Can you accept this?"

"Yes. Thank you," she said.

When Sarah came out of trance, Earle's eyes were red from tears and he hugged his wife for a long time.

"If you want to remain with your wife and children,

you're going to have to find the self-discipline to act, Earle. How can you do that?"

He responded to me while looking at his wife. "Refuse to see or talk to Julie."

(NOTE: Any important relationship in this life probably relates back to one or more past-life relationships. I have no doubt that we could have explored Earle's past ties with Julie and Sarah.)

Nicole:
Seminar Dialogue

"My husband ran off with my best friend, leaving me with three kids," Nicole said. Her tone registered cool disapproval. "And you're telling me not to blame?"

"But that's what you wanted him to do, Nicole," I replied, toying with her.

"You're crazy," she said, shaking the microphone at me.

"Want to explore it in regression?"

"Sure," she said tersely.

Nicole went quickly into trance. I directed her back to the cause of her marital breakup. "Speak up and tell me what you perceive."

"Fire! There's fire. My boat's on fire. Tell the men." Nicole's voice was agitated and she was trembling.

"What's happening now?" I asked.

"Leavin' ... before I burn my arse. Rowin' into the dark."

"Are the men with you in the rowboat?"

"Nah."

"Are they still on the burning boat?"

"Yeah."

"Are there more rowboats for them?"

51

"Nah."

"You said, 'my boat.' Are you the captain?"

"So what?"

"Did you abandon your men, Captain?"

"So what? They're just scum."

From Higher Self, I asked Nicole to talk to me about how the past life related to her present situation.

"Eighteen men died in the boat fire. I am beginning to resolve my karma by learning what it means to be abandoned. My present bitterness about Jack's leaving me shows I've learned nothing. Unless I can forgive him for leaving me and forgive myself for what I did, I will continue to experience similar situations in this life and future lives. Blythe, my best friend who ran off with Jack, was one of the men on the ship."

 *"I've seen it happen. Having to cope with the pressures of success. There are plenty of negatives."*

Chapter Five
NEGATIVE PAYOFF

A negative payoff is a situation in which you say you want something to be different than it is, but consciously or subconsciously, you block the desired goal because there is a payoff in maintaining the status quo. A good example of this was a woman in a seminar who said she desired to be wealthy. She worked hard and used programming techniques to support her goals. Yet when I began to process her, it became obvious she was subconsciously blocking her own success out of love for her father. If she allowed herself to "show him up," he would be hurt and she would experience the guilt.

In another case, a woman claimed she wanted to find a husband. But she was extremely overweight and did nothing to make herself more attractive. During processing, she said a mate would be possessive—restricting her activities and complicating her life. "I'm not too fond of fixing meals on schedule, or washing and ironing either," she added. Obviously, no matter how much she talked about wanting to get married, there was a bigger payoff in remaining single.

Action Required

Explore your goals and desires. Ask yourself two questions: "If I get what I say I want, what will change?" and "What are the potential undesirable changes?" The negative payoffs will be in number two.

Hollis:
Seminar Dialogue

Hollis raised his hand for the microphone. When he received it, he stood and looked at the floor for a while as if to build anticipation. He was dressed in a cotton sport coat, a T-shirt, and jeans. "I'm trying to see the negative payoff in my failed business ventures," he finally said.

"Tell me about them, Hollis."

"Oh, I've tried so many things, but they never work. Car washes, hamburger stands ... you name it."

"What do you really find joy in doing?"

"Writing. I'm a free-lance writer and I love it. It's just that it doesn't pay enough. I have to find a way to make more money," he said solemnly.

"You're a good writer? You do it naturally and well? It's fun?"

"Absolutely!"

"If your other businesses were to succeed, would they reduce or eliminate your writing time?"

"Yes, but ... oh-h-h-h!" A flash of understanding shot across Hollis's face.

"You don't dare let yourself succeed then, do you?" He slowly nodded his head in agreement. "Why not focus your energy on finding new ways to make money writing, instead of assuming a limitation?"

He flashed a thumbs up signal as he sat down.

Negative Payoff
Seminar Process

"Life is a game," I said to the group. "Some people play it as a game of struggle, or sickness, or poverty, or being right all the time. We're all playing a game we set up. And if your games were not bringing you some kind of payoff, you'd stop playing. It will always serve you to explore the secret satisfaction you receive from not being fully in charge of any aspect of your life. As an example, if you feel like you are victimized, you're receiving some satisfaction from being a victim. If you are weak, or poor, or inadequate, there is a payoff of some kind in it for you. Negative games can be great attention getters, and they often protect you from blame. There are an infinite number of games. To name a few: I can't find the right relationship game. My relationship is miserable game. I can only attain a limited level of success game. I never have enough money game. I'm from a dysfunctional family game. I don't have the talent game.

"If you want to stop playing games you can't win, it takes time, energy and commitment. You need to discover what's blocking you ... what's keeping you from changing. Often the block is a negative payoff. In the process I'm going to conduct, I'll be asking you a lot of questions. I want you to be aware of your very first response to each question ... the response that just bubbles up from deep within you."

(NOTE: Readers of this volume can simply answer the questions, or if you'd prefer to explore the questions in an

altered state, make your own self-hypnosis tape. My book, **Finding Your Answers Within,** *[Pocket Books] explains how.)*

As an altered-state process, I hypnotized the seminar participants and when the induction was complete, I said, "Let's explore the concept of negative payoffs as they relate to getting what you want in life. We'll begin with your primary relationship. If you were to have what you really want in your primary relationship, what changes would be required on your part?"

(Pause)

"Are any of these changes undesirable? If so, you may have found a negative payoff for keeping things the way they are."

(Pause)

"All right, let's explore another area. If you were to get what you really want in regard to your relationship with your family and friends, what changes would be required on your part?"

(Pause)

"Are any of these changes undesirable? If so, you may have found a negative payoff for keeping things the way they are."

(Pause)

"Okay, now let's explore another area. If you were to get what you really want in regard to your career and level of success, what changes would be required on your part?"

(Pause)

"Are any of these changes undesirable? If so, you may have found a negative payoff for keeping things the way they are."

(Pause)

"All right, let's explore another area. If you were to get what you really want in regard to how you spend your time, what changes would be required on your part?"

(Pause)

"Are any of these changes undesirable? If so, you may have found a negative payoff for keeping things the way they are."

(Pause)

"If you were to create the healthy, attractive body you desire, what changes would be required on your part?"

(Pause)

"Are any of these changes undesirable? If so, you may have found a negative payoff for keeping things the way they are."

(Pause)

"Okay, I'm now going to give you a few minutes to meditate upon your clarity of intent. Do you really want to change? Can you see how your negative payoffs are blocking you from experiencing the self-discipline and self-esteem you really desire?"

(Pause)

The participants were awakened and I asked for volunteers to share what they experienced in the process.

Sharon:
Seminar Dialogue

"I didn't have any trouble with the changes required to achieve more career success, but I came to understand that if I were to get what I want, I'd probably feel guilty about it, and maybe even do something to destroy it," Sharon said.

"Why would you feel guilty about being successful?" I asked.

"I don't think I've paid enough dues?"

"That's a faulty assumption that will keep you from succeeding. But there's more to it. What will change in your life if you are successful?"

"I'm an actress, and I work a day job as a waitress. But I know if I got a good part, my friends would be jealous, especially those who are better than me." Sharon winced, as if speaking the words made her uncomfortable.

"What else would change?"

"I'd be able to buy some new clothes."

"Changes that you *wouldn't* like?" I said, stressing the word "wouldn't."

"Maybe losing my friends. I've seen it happen. Having to cope with the pressures of success. There are plenty of negatives. Working twelve hours or more a day if I were to get a part on a series. I'd have to come home and study my lines for the next day. It's the end of any personal life. I don't know how or if my boyfriend would adjust."

"Have you made yourself clear?" I asked.

"Yikes," she said, then paused. "Maybe the idea of 'paying my dues' is just a matter of stalling off something I don't really want?"

 *"But if I were direct and honest with some people, they would hate me."*

Chapter Six

MASKS OR ACTS

There are three ways to generate change in a human being:

1. Add something to their life: people, things, environment, awareness, programming, challenge, et cetera.

2. Subtract something from their life: people, things, environment, challenge, et cetera.

3. Get the person to be who they really are. This is transcendental change. Accepting what is in yourself is the beginning of transformation, because you can't change what you don't recognize.

Whenever you wear masks, you are attempting to avoid pain. You think the real you isn't adequate enough, or impressive enough, or kind enough, or loving enough, so you pretend to be more than you are. Maybe you're afraid of hurting someone's feelings so you wear a nice mask. Or you're insecure about your job so you wear a sincere and dependable mask. A gregarious mask is good to deflect real contact, avoid intimacy, or hide insecurity. There are thousands of masks.

Masks are repressions, which is fear. There is no way to successfully repress who you are. It's like holding a rubber life raft under water. As long as you're willing to exert effort, you can do it, but eventually you're going to get tired and the raft will surface. A man represses his anger with his wife, but takes it out on his employees. A woman wears a fake smile all day at work; her repression takes the form of an ulcer. For years a man checks his emotional desires and the repression manifests as cancer. Repressed feelings will always come out.

Action Required

1. Understand why you wear the mask. What is the fear behind the false face? 2. Decide if the reason you wear it is valid anymore. Often it isn't. 3. Analyze the cost of wearing your mask. In other words, how is the resulting repression manifesting in your life? 4. Realize that all you have to do to remove your mask is be direct and honest in your communications with others.

Erica:
Seminar Dialogue

"But if I were direct and honest with some of the people in my life, they would hate me," said Erica. She was a woman in her early fifties. Her attire would have been appropriate for an executive office.

"What you're saying, Erica, is they would hate you unless they can manipulate you to be what they want you to be instead of what you are." I paused to let the reality of the statement sink in. "Do you need people like that in your life?"

"Oh-h-h-h! I see what you mean. Okay, let me ask you something else. I always have to act like I'm in control. It's almost more important than anything else in my life. Is that a mask?

"Are you always in control?"

"Of course not, but I'm not about to let anyone else know that," she replied, straightening her shoulders and clearing her throat.

"The real you is sensitive, vulnerable, and not always sure about the best way to handle things?" I asked lightly.

Her response was an amused nod.

"Then what is the cost of repressing who you really are?"

"The cost? Hm-m-m-m ... I probably scare a lot of people off, such as men I'd really like to know and get close to. And I have to spend a lot of time alone to recharge myself enough to go back out there and play the role of ..."

"Superwoman?" I interrupted. She chuckled. "Let's look for the cause, Erica." She agreed and was quickly in deep hypnosis. I directed her back to the events responsible for her current need to appear in control.

"I'm in woods ... dense woods and shells are exploding all around us. There's a cannon ... old-fashioned type of ... I'm so confused. So confused. I just don't know what to do." Her voice was deep and strained.

"Are you in command?"

"I am now. The captain's dead."

"All right ... let's move forward a little way into the future so you can tell me what happens. One, two, three."

"It was terrible. I let the men try to save themselves. We lost the position and the Germans broke through. Most of our men died. I could have saved many of them by grouping at the hilltop ... and we could have held it."

From her Higher Self perspective, I asked Erica to share her understanding. "I wasn't trained in that life to take command. I did the best I knew how, but I wasn't very effective. Now I must separate the past from the present. No one will die today if I am not in control of the situation. My subconscious is shielding me from re-experiencing the guilt and pain of a time I didn't take control."

Terrance:
Seminar Dialogue

"People who reinvent themselves know the value of high self-esteem," I said to the group. "And they refuse to do anything that lowers it. Basic to this is the idea of being direct and honest in your communications with other people. Don't lie, and don't fake what you feel. Don't say yes when you want to say no. Don't pretend to care when you don't. Don't spend time with people who don't enhance your life. Don't pretend to accept liberal ideas to win acceptance if you're really a conservative. In other words, don't wear a mask. Masks always lower self-esteem."

"What about wearing a heterosexual mask when you really want to experience homosexuality?" Terrance asked. He was in his mid-thirties, dressed casually in a patterned silk shirt and Levi's, and obviously insecure about asking the question.

"It's repression, the same as the other examples we've talked about. So it's fear. So there is a price to pay for not expressing your true sexuality."

"I wonder if the disapproval that will result will be worth the pleasure," Terrance said. "My parents would be devastated. My co-workers would titter behind my back. My old friends would probably disappear."

"I don't have an answer for you, Terrance. Those are things you'll have to weigh. But I will point out that esoteric metaphysics, as it is taught in Wicca and other mystery school organizations, claims that when you repress what you are and what you desire to do, it generates a vibrational energy within your soul. This energy will have to be expressed, if not in this life, in the next. The repression of sexual energy can pervert the energy, causing it to be expressed in unhealthy ways. The large number of priests who have molested children is an example right out of today's headlines."

Terrance smiled. I continued. "Osho would say, 'If you feel the need to express your sexuality, it is God-given energy. That means there is something to be learned through the experience.'"

Eliza:
Seminar Dialogue

"I don't agree with what you just said to Terrance. To accept a gay lifestyle will turn his life and the lives of everyone who cares about him upside down," Eliza said. She was an attractive woman in her early thirties. She held the microphone with one hand and her husband's hand with the other.

"For Terrance to repress his sexuality won't make it go away," I said.

"Most spiritual teachers advise that you transmute your sexual energy and focus it upon spiritual concerns."

"Most spiritual teachers are loony," I replied. "Transmute is a fancy word for repression in the real world. In a spiritual cult, someone who eats a cosmic foo-foo diet and chants a few hours a day will quell their sexual energy along with the rest of their mental functions. In time they'll only respond to command."

"Obviously, you're not very spiritual," she said scowling.

"I am whatever you think I am. There's no way I could be anything else to you. But if you want to move past sex, I'll have to agree with William Blake, who said, 'The road to excess leads to the palace of wisdom.' In other words, from the perspective of long-term harm, repression is worse than indulgence, because you will eventually get tired of what you indulge in."

Gillian:
Seminar Dialogue

"Masks are always created and worn to keep out the pain and to avoid loss. But that also keeps out the joy. If you aren't living a fulfilled life you could be deflecting the joy," I said to the group. "Change begins with action. Action starts by finding out who you are behind your masks, and by understanding your fears. You can't change what you don't recognize.

"The underlying philosophy behind the human-potential movement is one of openness and honesty. The idea is to express your feelings and open up areas long dormant and maybe painful, with the faith that in so doing you will release a great potential for creativity and joy."

I scanned the group, making eye contact with as many people as possible. Then putting up my hand, I said, "How many of you sometimes put other people's self-interest before your own? Maybe you put your kids first, or your parents, or people in need, or your social causes."

Ninety percent of the seminar participants raised their hands.

"That's the 'fool yourself' mask," I said.

"I resent that," Gillian said. She was in her late thirties or early forties, with luminous auburn hair that reached her waist. She was wearing Melrose Avenue style designer clothes. "I've done some things I'm not very proud of to make the extra money it has taken to support my mother in a nursing home for the last eleven years."

"Really?"

"I work for an escort service," she said. "That's a nice way of saying I sell my body."

"What would you think of yourself, Gillian, if you hadn't done everything you could to take care of your sick mother?"

"I couldn't have lived with it. I'd rather have died. That's why I've been willing to do what I've done."

"So you did it for yourself, not your mother. To not have done what you've done would have been the equivalent of dying."

She didn't respond, so I continued. "Everyone is selfish. So what? Everyone acts in their own self-interest all the time. So what? Just stop fooling yourself about why you do what you do. Never play a martyr. In claiming to be selfless you gain enormously in self-esteem, but it's a matter of fooling yourself. To those who are aware, selfless claims are always self-renunciation."

Chapter Seven

INCOMPATIBLE GOALS AND VALUES

If your goals and values are not compatible, you will either subconsciously block yourself from achieving your goals or you'll change your values to make them consistent with your goals. A third possibility is that you'll destroy one or the other in the process. As an example, if your wife and family are your highest value, and your goal is to become a manufacturer's representative covering a five-state territory, your value and goal are inconsistent. Your work would necessitate travel, allowing minimal home life.

Action Required

Recognize the incompatible goals and values. List your goals, one to ten, with the most important at the top. Do the same with your values. Any great separation on the list will indicate that you need to rethink one or the other, to resolve or avoid a conflict.

Seminar Process Sheet

Which areas of your life create the most value for you? Many general areas are listed below, and you may think of more. Choose eight that relate to your priorities and list them in order of importance. One is the most important and eight least important. You will defeat the purpose of this process unless you answer honestly. List the life areas in their **real** order of value to you, **not** in the order you or your mate *think* they should be.

Your Life Values

Mate/Love relationship
Mate/Children/Family
Work/Career/Profession
Friends/Relatives
Physical fitness/Exercise
Beauty-related concerns
Home environment
Material possessions
Finances/Success
Hobbies

Creative activities
Education/Intellectual
    development
Recreation/Play/Leisure
Spirituality/Expanding
    Awareness
Community involvement
Service to causes and
    Volunteer work
Other

1. _____
2. _____
3. _____
4. _____
5. _____
6. _____
7. _____
8. _____

Your Goals

Primary short-term career goal _____

Long-term career goal _____

Primary short-term personal goal _____

Long-term personal goal _____

Relationship goal _____

Other goals _____

_____

_____

Are your most important goals and values compatible? Examples: If your #1 value is Physical fitness/Exercise, and your primary personal goal is to run a marathon, your goal and value are aligned. If your primary personal goal is to become a successful artist and you paint during free time at home, the goal is compatible with any of the home-based primary values. But if your primary personal goal is to run a small day-care center and your #1 value is material possessions, the goal may not be capable of generating enough to fulfill your monetary expectations.

Justin:
Seminar Dialogue

"When I listed my life area values in the last group process, they were: 1. spirituality, 2. friends/associates, 3. community involvement, 4. education/intellectual development, 5. physical fitness/well-being, and 6. recreation/leisure activities," Justin explained, looking at me in confusion.

"So?" I said. "You're not very materialistic, are you?"

"So, the following didn't even make my list—finances,

career, emotions/love/sex, family life, physical environment, or material possessions. But on my list of goals, the top one is a million dollars."

I laughed. "Who's fooling who, Justin?"

"I've been saying 'I want to make a million' to myself and everyone else for five years," he said seriously.

"Then it's time to stop fooling yourself, isn't it? If you want to make a million dollars, you've got to enjoy the game you play to attain the money, and you'd better have an emotional purpose behind the goal."

"What do you mean, 'an emotional purpose'?"

"Oh, fame, or glory, or to send your children to Harvard, or to impress the woman that you want to marry. Something like that," I said. "If your goal is practical, when the going gets tough you'll tend to reduce the goal rather than forge ahead. Which are you willing to rethink, Justin, your goals or values?"

"Not my values," Justin quickly replied. His eyes grew openly amused, he smiled and sat down. "I don't know what I'd do with a million dollars if I had it," I heard him say to the person sitting beside him.

 *"If you think I'm going to stop trying to change him, you're crazy."*

Chapter Eight
RESISTANCE TO "WHAT IS"

It is your resistance to "what is" that causes your suffering. Freedom lies in the acceptance of what is, for when you recognize and accept things as they are, you stop wasting mental or physical energy attempting to change what cannot be changed. This is simple logic. There are things you have a potential to change, so go ahead and change them. Do everything you can to bring about the change. But there are also things you cannot change, so recognize these areas of your life and stop wasting your efforts. Most importantly, stop generating negative subconscious programming with your frustrations.

A Christian prayer says the same thing: "God grant me the serenity to accept the things I cannot change, the courage to change the things I can, and the wisdom to know the difference."

Action Required

Accept the facts, logic, and unalterable realities in your life. Actually, you have no choice but to accept what is. You only have a choice in how you respond to what is.

Arlene:
Seminar Dialogue

Arlene, an attractive woman in her mid-forties, raised her hand to share. When she received the microphone, she said, "For twenty-five years I've been attempting to change my husband. He's so quiet it's almost impossible to get him to talk, and when he does he's sarcastic.

"Every night after work, he stops for a drink at the bar with his friends. He constantly has me upset. Now, it sounds like you're saying to accept him just the way he is."

"*He* has upset you by being what he is?"

"He certainly has," she responded in a grudging voice. "If he was nicer to me and came home right after work, I'd be happier. If you think I'm going to stop trying to change him, you're crazy."

"Nothing has happened in twenty-five years. How long do you think it's going to take?" I asked, unable to suppress a smile.

"I just don't know."

"Arlene, how many hours of your marriage have you spent being upset over the way your husband is?"

"I don't know. Thousands, I suppose. Once I threatened to leave him unless he quit stopping at the bar. He did for two weeks, but he made my life so miserable it wasn't worth it." She sighed and slumped in a sympathy-seeking gesture.

"Arlene, your husband has never made you miserable. You've made yourself needlessly miserable for twenty-five years by resisting what he is. Plus, you've generated a lot of negative subconscious programming which has manifested as additional disharmony in your life."

"So you think I should give up after all this time?" she said, disbelief in her voice.

"Well, it seems to me you have three choices, Arlene. You can leave him. You can keep resisting him and be miserable. Or, if you're going to stay with him, accept him for what he is and spend your emotional energy constructively for a change. Your life will get better immediately because the negative self-programming will stop. If you change, he might even respond differently to the new, nice you. Don't be blind to the logic."

"But that would be admitting I've wasted twenty-five years."

"You have, Arlene. Your husband was perfect all along, and you didn't know it.

"*Perfect*?" Her voice was sarcastic and her brows furrowed in an angry frown.

"Since you now realize you can't change him, doesn't it make sense to accept him as he is? It's simple logic. And if you accept him as he is, he's perfect from your perspective. You can't accept him and not accept him at the same time. Besides, unless you accept him, you'll have to come back together in similar circumstances in a future life."

Arlenes's frown deepened, but she didn't respond, so I continued. "Your husband is your karma. He's here to teach you to accept what is. Isn't that nice?" I flashed a large, friendly smile.

"You're as bad as he is," she said, sitting down.

Derrick:
Seminar Dialogue

"When you refuse to accept what is, you *deny reality,*" I said. "The idea is to accept what is and let unalterable situations flow through you without affecting you."

"How can you deny the reality of an eroding social system without getting upset?" Derrick asked, raising one hand in a gesture of futility. He had long hair tied back in a ponytail and was dressed in jeans, a T-shirt and cotton sport coat.

"Obviously it's your viewpoint that our social system is eroding. It's not necessarily my viewpoint," I said.

"We can no longer count on the basic foundations of society," he said, sweeping his hand to include the hotel ballroom. "Banks, insurance companies, and the social system are a screwed up mess. Add to that gang violence, drugs, homelessness, and a declining school system. That, my friend, adds up to an eroding reality."

"Maybe a reality of chaos will be more workable in some ways. Maybe the changes will lead to new and better systems," I said smiling. Derrick became upset.

"These things don't upset you?" he said, his voice angry.

"What can I, as an individual, do about them?" I asked.

"Plenty. If we were all a little more socially concerned, we could do plenty."

"Derrick, even the government with its manpower and money printing press doesn't seem to be able to do much about our unworkable systems. Sure, I can vote in support of my beliefs, contribute to our local school and to homeless causes, and I do. My wife volunteers a lot of time to our kid's school because there isn't enough state money to make the classrooms work. But this is what is. Getting upset about these things won't change them. I have to be responsible first to my family and myself. At the end of the week, I might have a few extra hours left over. If I used my little remaining free time and energy trying to change the social system, what good would it do? I'd be frustrated, exhausted, and miserable. The reality is, we are in the middle of massive changes that are driving us forward into new futures."

"We've traded stability for chaos."

"No, what we thought was stable wasn't, and chaos has become an operative concept for trying to understand our relationship to the totality—global earth. We have to learn to be responsive to the interconnectedness of the whole, and to recognize all the new opportunities that will emerge."

"I can't deal with it."

"You don't have any choice, Derrick. Get it? What is, is. You can fight it, hate it, and waste all your energy resisting it. Chaos doesn't care, and you make yourself miserable." He sighed. I continued. "Maybe your mistake is in believing you have a responsibility to bring order and reason into our social system."

He shrugged his shoulders.

"What if you were to give up the illusion that order is necessary for your safety and peace of mind?" I asked.

He nodded again and sat down.

Margaret:
Seminar Dialogue

"What a defeatist attitude," Margaret said, glaring at me. "Derrick is unwilling to accept the status quo. He wants to do his part to bring society into balance and you put him down."

In her late twenties or early thirties, Margaret was a long-haired blonde, wearing jeans and two layers of tank tops. She looked over at Derrick who was sitting in the row behind her.

I smiled. "Derrick wants to fix the banks, insurance companies, gangs, drugs, homelessness, and the school system."

"Right," she said.

"He's making himself miserable by resisting what is."

"Damned right," she almost shouted. "Everyone in this room should be sharing his concerns."

"What do you resist most in our declining system, Margaret?"

"Corporations."

"All corporations?"

"Yes. They fleece the people, take all the money and use it for their own selfish purposes."

"Give me an example of one corporation."

Margaret named a Los Angeles film company, and explained that she worked in a secretary pool. "I've been there three years. I know how it works."

"And they aren't paying you enough?" I asked.

"That's part of it. A little respect might also be in order," she said, twisting the microphone cord into a knot with her free hand.

"Are your co-workers treated differently?"

"No, we're all in the same boat."

"Do they also resist what is about the film studio?"

"Most of them just accept the way it is."

"What would you have them do, Margaret?"

"We should probably organize and force them to pay us more and treat us better."

I taunted her by laughing. "You want to organize a secretaries union?" The participants laughed too.

Margaret scowled more. "It could be done."

"Maybe. If you're willing to turn your entire life into a crusade. And nobody is going to pay you to do it." I paused. "I always suggest that you spend your time wisely, because you only have so much of it."

She didn't respond, so I continued. "You have expectations that are in conflict with what is, Margaret. The film company pays a basic wage and has an employment policy. They don't care if you quit, because there are hundreds of other young women out there who are willing to take your place. That's what is."

"So I'm supposed to just accept it."

"As I've already pointed out several times in this seminar, you don't have any choice. You can choose to quit or stay, and you can choose to resist what is, or not resist what is. That's it. SO GET OFF IT. Instead of wasting your energy and creating more negativity, you could be focusing your energy on something positive, such as learning a craft that would pay better, or starting your own business."

She scowled at me without responding.

"Of course, you always have the free will to be self-destructive," I added.

"My pride would never allow me to accept your stupid teachings," she said, dropping the microphone and walking out of the seminar.

Chapter Nine
MIRRORING

The positive or negative qualities you react to in others are a reflection of the same qualities within you. Other people are a mirror for you; if you are aware, you can learn from the mirror. If you see fear in someone else, you're recognizing fear within yourself. If you think someone is selfish and it bothers you, be aware there is selfishness within you. Any quality in another person that really bothers or attracts you, exists within yourself as well.

Action Required

Examine your reactions to others by searching yourself for the corresponding traits. If your reaction is negative, it is rooted in a fear, which you are here on earth to resolve. See the people you dislike as mirrors instead of adversaries.

Spencer:
Seminar Dialogue

"I'm having a hard time with that concept, Richard,"

Spencer said. His arms were crossed tightly across his chest, one hand raised just enough to hold the microphone. "I'm really bothered by the irrational actions of some of the world's leaders. They certainly aren't a mirror for me."

"You're never irrational?" I asked.

"Well ... yes, but not on that scale. Their actions affect millions," he said.

"Scale has nothing to do with it. When were you most irrational?"

He hesitated, then replied. "During my divorce, I suppose. Okay, got it. But what about an attention seeker? There is a flamboyant woman in our office who literally drives me crazy. She has to have attention, and if she can't get it one way, she'll find another. She wears wild clothes, crazy hats, and brings in beautifully decorated birthday cakes for staffers. If you don't go out of your way to acknowledge her, she does something to attract your attention. Now I don't see myself in her—I'm quiet and go out of my way to avoid attracting attention."

"No way, Spencer. If you're that bothered by her, you really need to attract attention in some area of your life," I said. "What do you do for a living?"

"I'm an advertising agency art director."

"Interesting. I'm quite familiar with art directors. And I've yet to meet a good one who didn't enter his best work in the annual art shows, hoping to take some awards. Awards are great ego boosters, they enhance your reputation in the field and get you a higher salary when you move on to your next job. It's a more subtle way of getting attention, but ..."
I stood looking at Spencer, without saying anything.

"Well, sure. I want respect within the agency and in my

field."

"You'd really like to be thought of as one of the top art directors in Los Angeles, wouldn't you?"

"Of course."

"Why does this bother you?"

"It doesn't."

"Yes it does, Spencer, or you wouldn't be bothered by the attention seeker in your office."

He took a deep breath and expelled it with a gusty sigh. Keeping his arms crossed on his chest, he looked at the floor, then frowned at me. "Well, the ad field is obsessed with who's hot, what concepts are hot, who can steal whose account, and who takes the most awards in this year's show. It gets old. Once you have a reputation, it's a never-ending battle to retain it."

"So you let your creative work attract attention and enhance your reputation. In her way, the woman in your office uses wild clothes and birthday cakes to do the same thing. She's a mirror for your fear of maintaining your reputation."

Spencer silently mouthed a four-letter word as he sat down.

Seminar Process

This process is conducted with the seminar participants in an altered state of consciousness.

"All right, I'm going to ask you to look into the mirror. Be honest and open to expanding your awareness of how you see yourself mirrored in others. First, think of a very important past relationship that ended negatively."

(Pause)

"How does the negativity in the other person mirror itself in you? Be open to all the possibilities and potentials."

(Pause and repeat, exploring another past relationship that ended negatively.)

"Okay, now think of the one other person on the planet who bothers you more than anyone else. And explore how their negativity reflects within you."

(Pause)

"All right, now think of one of your present relationships that contains negativity. And explore how the negativity in the other person is mirrored within you."

(Pause)

"Now let's look at the positive side of the mirror. Think of someone you like or admire. And explore how their positive character traits reflect in you."

(Pause)

Lilian:
Seminar Dialogue

"In that last process, the person who bothers me more than anyone else is President Bush. Instead of focusing his power on things that needed to be handled in this country, he concentrated on international issues," Lilian said. She was in her late thirties, overweight and casually dressed.

"You never focus your energy upon the wrong priorities?" I asked.

Lilian's husband, sitting beside her, smiled broadly and nodded.

"Then you also think Bush's priorities were wrong?" she asked.

"I didn't say that. And you're avoiding my question."

She considered for a moment, then said, "I handle my priorities according to their importance."

"Do you think President Bush handled the national and international priorities according to his idea of their importance?"

"Probably, but I think history will show he was wrong."

"Does everyone in your life agree with the way you order your priorities?"

Lilian looked down at her husband and paused as a flash of recognition crossed her face. "No, Jack thinks I should put him a little higher on my list."

Jack laughed and said, "Thanks."

Chapter Ten

FEAR

Fear is a big word. All disturbances between human beings, large or small, interpersonal or international, are rooted in fear. Fear means all the negative emotions such as anger, selfishness, jealousy, prejudice, hate, repression, envy, possessiveness, greed, anxiety, guilt, insecurity, depression, inhibitions, vanity, malice, resentment, blame, et cetera. The fears work against your spiritual evolution, and they can paralyze you, keeping you from acting when you need to act—keeping you from making a growth choice when it would be in your best interest.

Action Required

Discover the cause of the fear if possible. Next, work to rise above the effects of the fear by examining it in the light of reality. When measured logically and from a self-actualized, metaphysical perspective, the fear will prove to be a delusion. Although a delusion, if caused by repressed anger (as is often the case with anxiety, guilt, and depression), it's often necessary to express your true feelings as a first step in releasing the anger. In other fear-based situations, it is of value to confront the fear by gathering the courage to act despite your desire to play it safe.

Marilyn:
Seminar Dialogue

"I'm very possessive of my husband and I understand that it's a fear of losing him. But he has never done anything to make me feel insecure in any way," Marilyn said. She was attractive, in her early thirties, and dressed in white cotton beach attire.

"Are you possessive about other people in your life?" I asked. "Are you possessive of material possessions?"

"No, not of people or things," she replied. "That's why it just doesn't make any sense. But it's there. And I'm not just a little possessive. I'm *really* possessive."

Marilyn agreed to use regressive hypnosis to go back to the cause of her possessiveness. After directing her through time I asked her to relate her understanding to me.

"I'm on a dock. The harbor is filled with old sailing ships and there are people dressed in funny clothes. Oh. I'm saying goodbye to someone. Ah ... I think he's my fiance. Yes, he is dressed as a sailor and he's kissing me goodbye."

"How long will he be gone?"

"I don't know. A long time. But we're going to get married when he comes home."

"All right, move forward in time until something important happens in regard to your relationship."

"I don't believe it. I don't believe it." Her voice was pained. "I waited over a year for him, counting the days.

And now his mates tell me he jumped ship and married a woman in England." Tears began running down her cheeks.

After directing her into her Higher Self, I asked her to explain her possessiveness.

"Obviously, I am afraid since he left me once, he will do it again. But I need to realize that my fear could create a problem where none exists. The tighter I attempt to hold onto him, the more he will want to be free. I'm also getting that it would be a karmic mistake to do something to even the score in this lifetime."

Seminar Case History

To make a point during the seminar, I related a case of false-fear karma. "The woman was divorced, but she could not let go of her ex-husband and allow herself to get involved with a new man. Every time she started to get serious about someone, her ex-husband filled her mind until it destroyed the new relationship.

"So I regressed her back to the cause. She found herself in the Middle Ages. Her husband was older, and she fell in love with his brother. They had an affair, and she got pregnant. When the woman's husband found out, he publicly tortured them both, cut out their tongues, and hanged them."

I paused to let the words sink in. "Her husband in that life is her ex-husband in this life. Subconsciously, she fears he'll do it again, but this isn't the Middle Ages and he's not in a position of power. The fear isn't valid in the present context."

Jodie:
Seminar Dialogue

"You say anger is a fear-based emotion." Jodie looked at

me. I nodded and she continued, "Well, I can't quite accept that. I mean, I get angry a dozen times a day, and it has nothing to do with being afraid."

I guessed Jodie to be in her late forties. She had flaming red hair, an outgoing personality and a fashion-model figure.

"Give me an example of getting angry," I said.

"If someone cuts me off on the freeway, I get furious."

"What do you do when this happens? Do you honk at them or give them the finger?" I asked.

"Nothing. I certainly don't want to get shot."

"So you don't vent the anger and it builds up until it turns against you."

"What do you mean, it turns against me?"

"Anger generates more anger, which generates more anger. Pretty soon you're so full of anger, every little situation becomes a big deal. You probably build a little anger into a big fantasy response, right? You imagine horrible things happening to the person who has offended you."

Jodie nodded and smiled sheepishly. "Something like that. But what does that have to do with fear?"

"There are many ways to look at the fear—the fear of not having your rights respected, or the fear of not getting your way. Anger is a standard response to not getting what you want. You wanted other drivers to respect your space, but you were cut off and you got mad. But everybody gets cut off on the freeway once in a while. You've probably accidentally cut people off yourself. Being cut off really isn't the problem. The problem is twofold. First, you have expectations that are in conflict with what is. Freeways are full of asshole drivers. That's what is. Accept it. Second, you repressed your anger rather than expressing it."

"How? By giving the guy the finger and having him pull a gun?"

"Anger is hurt that hasn't been expressed. Even if you have no right to feel hurt, until you release the anger through expression it will build up and fester inside you. Obviously, the freeway is no place to express anger. The odds are probably a million to one against anyone shooting you, but you might cause an accident." I paused and looked directly into her eyes. "But, in most situations that cause you to get angry, you could express your hurt directly and honestly, couldn't you?"

Jodie nodded. "Sometimes I feel like I'm about ready for a straitjacket. I have one angry response after another, all day long."

"And in response, how often do you say what you want to say?"

"Hardly ever."

"Then from this moment on, start expressing your hurt. Forget about the other person's reactions. What's important is that you release it."

Jodie was about to say something and I interrupted her. "Anger preoccupies you and keeps you from being able to focus your energy upon positive things. So the idea is to understand anger for what it is. As you become more self-actualized, you'll be less likely to respond to irrational feelings, but until then, don't repress what you feel."

DeAndre:
Seminar Dialogue

"I'm really resentful about my girlfriend lying to me about seeing an old boyfriend," DeAndre said. He had long

95

dark hair, was in his late twenties and dressed for the L.A. club scene.

"What happened?"

"She told me she was going to spend the evening with her girlfriend, but instead she saw her old boyfriend who was in town for the weekend."

"Why didn't she tell you the truth?"

"Because she knew I'd freak out."

"Why? Were you afraid that she might like the old boyfriend better than you?"

"Yeah, well, not really."

"Your girlfriend knew you couldn't love her unconditionally, DeAndre. And you verified her assumption by admitting that you would have freaked out. And I'll bet you had quite a fight with her when you found out, didn't you?"

DeAndre shrugged and tapped his foot as if in time to unheard music, but he didn't respond.

"It's your problem, DeAndre. Resentment is a fear-based emotion. It's a matter of wanting things that happened in the past to have happened differently. Talk about a foolish expenditure of energy."

"Okay," he said.

"Your real problem is being unable to love unconditionally," I said. "Your parents didn't love and accept you unconditionally, did they?"

DeAndre laughed. "Far from it, man."

"So do you want to continue the pattern? Obviously, you're aware enough to attend a metaphysical/human-potential seminar. You understand that unconditional love is a matter of accepting another human being without judgment, blame or expectations?"

"Yes."

"If your girlfriend knew you loved her that way, she could have come to you and said, 'DeAndre, you might not understand this, but I'd like to talk to Tommy, my old boyfriend. He's only in town for the weekend. Would you mind?'"

"Man, it would be hard. I'd want to know why." DeAndre said.

"Well, the fact is, your girlfriend felt the need. She either wasn't complete with the relationship, or she wanted to compare her past choices to her present choice, or she just wanted to touch base with an old friend."

"As it worked out, it was probably all of the above."

"All the more reason to let go of the resentment," I said.

"Agreed," he said.

Seminar Fear-Block
Process #1

The following processes relate to anxiety and success. The questions promote self-exploration of fear blocks and assumed limitations, and are asked while the seminar participants are in an altered state of consciousness:

"Let's explore what would happen if you were to become very, very successful. Success changes things. Maybe if you were really successful it would change your relationship with your mate, friends or family. Maybe some of these changes are undesirable? Success often increases expectations, demands and pressures. And it can rob you of time you're used to spending in other areas. So, let's begin by meditating upon your success and what it would mean in regard to the important relationships in your life. Do this now."

(Two or three minutes of silence)

"If success means changing, are you willing to change?"

(Pause)

"All right, let's explore another aspect of success and fear. For many people, success generates a fear of ultimate failure at some future time. Does this relate to you? If you were to succeed, do you think it would cause you to be fearful of failure in the future? Meditate on this."

(Two or three minutes of silence)

"Okay, remember this, but let's move on and explore some more fears. You see, the fear of success, the fear of failure, the fear of being overwhelmed, and the fear of finishing all interact with each other and generate even greater fears and stresses.

"Let's explore the very common fear of failure. Does the fear of failure keep you from doing what you need to do, when you need to do it?"

(Pause)

"Do you feel that if you don't try, you can't fail?"

(Pause)

"Does what other people think reinforce this fear?"

(Pause)

"If you were to fail would it mean changes in your life that you aren't ready to accept? Meditate upon these questions."

(Two or three minutes of silence)

"All right, hopefully you are perceiving more fear blocks. Now, let's explore the fear of being overwhelmed. Do you avoid tasks because you think you might make mistakes?"

(Pause)

"Do you avoid tasks because you don't think you have

the ability to perform adequately?"

(Pause)

"Does the fear of being overwhelmed relate to any lack of self-discipline? Meditate upon these questions."

(Two or three minutes of silence)

"Another primary fear that often keeps you from doing what you need to do, when you need to do it, is the fear of finishing. Working on a particular project sets other factors into motion. Maybe you particularly enjoy an association with someone else on the project."

(Pause)

"Or maybe working on this task enhances your self-image."

(Pause)

"Or maybe the task provides a great excuse for you to avoid doing something you don't want to do. Meditate upon the fear of finishing."

(Two or three minutes of silence)

"All right, once again, remember everything you have come to realize about yourself in this process so that you can make notes immediately upon awakening. But now, meditate once again, and this time on the idea of any changes you need to make as a result of your realizations. What changes can you make that will increase your potential for success in all areas of your life?"

(Two or three minutes of silence)

Seminar Fear-Block
Process #2

"All right, it is time to face the fears that are creating blocks in your mind. In the preceding process we explored the fear of success, the fear of failure, the fear of being overwhelmed, and the fear of finishing. During the process you probably came up with several fears, and we're going to explore a couple of them now. First, choose one of your fears from the last process."

(Pause)

"Now, with this fear in mind,what is the worst that could happen if this fear were actualized? I want you to acknowledge this worst case scenario because a full awareness of your potential loss will clarify your anxiety. Meditate on this."

(Two or three minutes of silence)

"Okay, what would you do if the worst came to pass?"

(Pause)

"Where would you go for help?"

(Pause)

"How would you cope?"

(Pause)

"What would you do if the worst happened, *and then* what would you do? Meditate on these questions."

(Two or three minutes of silence)

"All right, now I'd like you to explore how you can reduce the likelihood of this undesirable event from occurring. What could you do to increase your safety? The more you can do, the less fearful you will be. You may also want to explore this from the perspective of how you can increase your chances of winning in this situation. Meditate on these things."

(Two or three minutes of silence)

"Now, choose another fearful realization you made in the preceding process. Remember, we explored the fear of success, the fear of failure, the fear of being overwhelmed, and the fear of finishing. Explore this realization."

(Repeat the questions above to explore the next realization.)

"Meditate upon the idea of any changes you need to make as a result of your realizations. What changes can you make that will increase your potential for success in all areas of your life?"

Chapter Eleven

THE NEED TO BE RIGHT

Your subconscious mind is a memory bank and operates very much like a computer. It's programmed for survival and for you to be "right." Everything you consider saying or doing is quickly run through your data banks, comparing the present to related past experiences. Your computer then approves your actions as compared to the past, for in the past you survived.

Computers are logically programmed machines and cannot be wrong. To be wrong is a malfunction. If your subconscious computer allowed you to be wrong, its survival is threatened. So, the only way it can work is to make you feel correct. It doesn't reason and it doesn't care if you get what you want out of life. It just needs to be right to protect itself, even if you lose the game.

Action Required

Learn to be aware of your programming so you can detach from the buttons that cause you to act like a robot. A robot has no choice in the way it acts. It has wiring and circuits that are set so when a button is pushed, it reacts according to programming. In many areas of your life you are programmed the same way. When your button is pushed you need to be right. Even if you're not right, you'll find some way to twist it around to justify yourself. Only those with enlightened awareness of how human beings work understand this. Winning the game is far more satisfying than getting to be right.

Anita:
Seminar Dialogue

"Can the need to be right come from past-life programming?" asked Anita, a pretty woman in her mid-twenties with large brown eyes and ultra-curly, brown hair. She was dressed in a silken pant suit.

"We're all programmed to need to be right, just as we are programmed to stand and walk on our feet," I replied. "But an excessive need to be right might go back to an event in past lives."

"But what do you do? My fiance has to be right about everything, all the time. No one else is ever right. It's enough to drive you nuts." She rolled her eyes at the ceiling and drew her lips in thoughtfully.

"Do you want to remain with him?"

"Of course. I love him."

"Then you'd better develop an enlightened attitude allowing him to be right while you win the game. You have to learn to override your own 'rightness' button. Knowing how he is programmed to function, you can let him be right. Remember, unless you allow him to be right, his survival is threatened and there is going to be trouble. So you can quickly allow him to be right with a phrase such as, 'Yes, John, I understand that.' You're not admitting he is right, you're just taking him off 'tilt.' His survival will no longer be threatened and he can concentrate upon the problem."

Jeff:
Seminar Dialogue

"I work for a computer software company in a support capacity," Jeff said. He was in his early thirties, had shoulder-length hair and was dressed in jeans and a sailing jacket. "In my training program I was taught never to try to be right, but not why, as you've just explained. When customers call they're usually at the end of their rope. Their computer is all messed up and they've probably been trying to get through on the phone for hours. You can imagine how mad they are. Threatened lawsuits are quite common."

I nodded, Jeff continued.

"So I agree with them. I say, 'You've got every right to be mad. I know I'd be furious in your place.' This calms them down enough to talk about the problem. Then, usually, I'm able to show them what they did to screw up the program, and they apologize and thank me before saying goodbye."

"And they're still loyal customers," I said.

Seminar Case History

"It's the seminar coordinator's job to have facial tissues on hand for participants who start crying," I explained. "Especially in the Bushido 'victim/bad guy' session when just about everyone cries. But at the last minute my coordinator realized she'd forgotten the boxes of tissues. She called hotel housekeeping, but the staff had gone home. She ran to the assistant manager and said, 'I have to have some boxes of facial tissue right away.' The assistant replied, 'Well you should have arranged that with housekeeping.' My coordinator let him be right, saying, 'I realize I should have done that, but I didn't. What can we do about it?'

"She could have argued with the manager, challenging his rightness. She could have reminded him how much we were paying for the ballroom, and how many seminar participants were staying in his hotel. But instead, she defused the situation by letting him be right. Then, she added, 'What can we do about it?' The moment the manager got what he needed, he could concentrate upon our need—the facial tissues. He raided the women's restroom supply locker and gave us six boxes of Kleenex."

 *"A woman certainly has a right to expect her husband to be faithful. After all, he vowed to be faithful at the marriage ceremony."*

Chapter Twelve
EXPECTATIONS

Expectations of a forthcoming experience will seldom serve you, for if the experience doesn't live up to your expectations, you'll be disappointed or unable to enjoy it for what it is.

Expectations of other people will never serve you. Whenever you expect someone else to be the way you want them to be, you're likely to be disappointed. No one can change someone else, nor can they expect another person to be anything other than what they are. When you insist that someone act according to your rules, they are forced to repress who they really are. Since long-term repression is impossible, the forced change will not last or it will result in new eruptions of unsatisfactory behavior.

Action Required

Attain a self-actualized perspective of the futility of expectations. Since it is impossible to change people, accept them as they are without resisting what is.

Kent:
Seminar Dialogue

"That's ridiculous. I just had lunch at a restaurant and the waitress was surly, and she brought me cold food. Since I'm paying for it, I certainly have a right to expect good service and warm food," Kent said with authority. He was in his late thirties and dressed in casual, trendy attire.

"But obviously your expectations were in conflict with what is. What did you do?" I asked.

"I got very angry. It turned into a terrible scene."

"And how do you feel about it right now?"

"I'm still upset."

"So, you've sent a lot of negative programming to your subconscious mind. What good did it do you, Kent?"

"What do you mean?"

"I mean what good did it do you? You got to be right, you caused a scene, and if you ate at all, you ate cold food. After the scene you probably felt uncomfortable. Maybe you got indigestion. What good did it do you?"

"I hope I got the waitress fired."

"A lot of good that did you. Maybe you got to 'be right,' but you didn't win the game. Now in addition to negative programming that will generate more negativity in your life, you missed lunch, experienced embarrassment and indigestion, and you may have created a karmic need to balance your conflict with the waitress. Maybe someday when you do something wrong, someone will cause a scene over it. Besides, that waitress usually isn't surly. She broke up with her boyfriend last night and as a result, she's depressed."

"Jeez-z-z-z," Kent exclaimed in frustration. "So what do you advocate, just taking crap from everybody?"

"I advocate that you be assertive and stand up for your human rights. But you made the whole situation worse for yourself. That's self-destructive. I'm sure five different enlightened people would have handled the situation five different ways, but they would have avoided being self-destructive."

"Give me an example." Kent said. His tone was coolly disapproving.

"You might have called the manager, calmly registered your complaints, refused to pay for lunch, then left."

"But I put up with rude service and received cold food."

"Right. And that's *what is*. Nothing was going to change that reality. You had two choices, resisting what is and making it worse for yourself, or accepting what is and handling the situation with minimal personal inconvenience."

"I see," he said slowly. "You always have the choice of making it better or worse. But I've always heard that if you feel anger, you shouldn't suppress it."

"I agree. But wisdom will eventually override your automatic anger response. Once you truly accept an enlightened perspective you won't choose anger because it won't serve you."

Kent nodded. The corners of his lips turned up in a slight smile. "Thanks," he said.

Amanda: Seminar Dialogue

"A woman certainly has a right to expect her husband to be faithful. After all, he vowed to be faithful at the marriage ceremony," Amanda said, her tone very emotional. She was

111

in her mid-thirties, attractive and dressed casually.

"Is your husband having an affair, Amanda?"

"He's had several, but he dismisses them as nothing serious."

"Have you had any affairs?"

"One to his dozen. And I only did it because he did."

"And you remain together?"

"Yes. Neither of us wants a divorce."

"So what is, is your husband is a man who has affairs. Your expectations of fidelity are in conflict with what is."

"Obviously. But it's not right. I want him to stop."

"You've discussed this with him. What has come out of the discussions?"

"He always says that he won't do it again, but he always does."

"Do you think he'll ever stop?"

"No."

"It seems to me you have three choices. 1. You can stop expecting fidelity and stay with him, knowing he will have affairs. 2. You can leave him and find another man who accepts monogamy. 3. You can make an agreement more in keeping with what is."

"What kind of agreement?"

"Whatever works for you. You could make multiple sexual partners—you, your husband and others—part of your lifestyle. That way it's a shared experience. Or you could explore responsible nonmonogamy or polyfidelity. There's..."

"None of those ideas are acceptable to me," she said scowling.

"Then you only have two choices."

"I just want him to be faithful."

"That's not a choice he's willing to make. You told us so yourself."

"Group sex is sinful."

"If you think something is sinful, whatever that means, then it is for you. Christian teachings would call it sinful. Are you a Christian?"

"No. I believe in New Age spirituality."

"Then why should you adhere to repressive Christian morality—guilt-inducing teachings devised to control parishioners? In Zen, the Three Pillars of Dharma contain five precepts of moral restraint. In the precept referring to sex, not committing sexual misconduct is defined as refraining from actions of sensuality which cause pain and harm to others, or turbulence or disturbance in ourselves."

I continued, "According to the Six Paramitas of the Bodhisattva, a person having sex with another must consider his own happiness, that of his companion and of the third person who will be most affected by his action. If these three concerned people can be satisfied, then the sex act comes under natural law and is completely acceptable."

"Who can say what is moral?" she asked.

"You, and only you, Amanda. Morality is a slippery, ever-changing concept. Please understand that I'm not trying to talk you into anything but accepting what is and letting go of your expectations."

Bobbi Sue:
Seminar Dialogue:

"Is it wrong to expect to have a life?" Bobbi Sue said. She was a sad-eyed woman in her mid-thirties, dressed in Levi's and a gingham blouse. "Being a single parent puts you at a tremendous disadvantage in our society. All the money I make goes to pay rent, bills and babysitters. And men aren't interested in taking on the responsibility of helping raise another man's child."

"Your life is the result of the choices you've made until now," I replied.

"I guess that's true. But I didn't know things would work out this way. I suppose it's my karma."

"And wisdom erases karma. Exactly what do you want?"

"I want a life."

"And the right man will give you a life?"

"Well ..." She looked away, then down at the floor. "I guess that's what it comes down to, doesn't it?"

"Nobody else can give you a life, Bobbi Sue. Obviously, a husband would help resolve the financial pressure, but a fulfilling life results from what you do and how you feel about it."

"Well, a husband would be a good start, but as I said, men aren't interested in taking on the responsibility of another man's child."

"That's a faulty assumption. Let's explore this from another perspective. You'll never find a lover who is more lovable than you are. Are you lovable, Bobbi Sue?"

"Huh?"

"Are you the lover you would want to love, if you were a man?"

She stalled, looked around the room and finally said, "No, probably not. I guess I'm pretty bitter. But I think I have a right to be."

I just stared at her.

"Okay," she said. "I've heard all the stuff you've said in

this seminar, and I know intellectually that you're right. But . . . ''

"Bobbi Sue!"

"Okay, okay.''

"Finding a mate isn't separate from creating a meaningful life, Bobbi Sue. You can find fulfillment in your career, and through loving your children, parents and friends. A sense of purpose provides fulfillment. Meanwhile, you can work on loving yourself and being lovable. You also have to be responsible to your goal, and position yourself to meet eligible men.''

"I guess my expectations are in conflict with what is, just as you said.'' She smiled sarcastically.

"You're right," I said. "What is, is you're bitter, unloving, and you find little that is meaningful in your daily life. Your expectations of finding a loving husband seem to be pretty unrealistic unless you're willing to change.''

Shrugging, she sat down.

Chapter Thirteen
CLARITY OF INTENT

The primary reason people are not as happy or successful as they desire to be is they are not clear on their intent. In other words, they don't know exactly what they want. If you don't know what you want, how do you expect to get it? In the seminars—even when people appear to be clear about what they want in life—when I process them, their confusion becomes obvious. All too often their wants are based upon what they think they *should* want, or what they think their friends or family want. Maybe they feel their real wants are greedy, so they disguise them. Others feel their real wants are irresponsible or unrealistic, so they won't admit to them.

Action Required

1. To unleash the unlimited power of your mind, you have to be honest with yourself about what you want. 2. Discover what is blocking you from getting what you want. It will be one of three things: a subconscious fear, a negative payoff, or a totally unrealistic goal. 3. Decide what you are willing

to pay to get what you want. The price will be one or more of the following: Time, effort, money, or sacrifice.

Once you have this awareness, you will decide to accomplish your goal or you will accept that it isn't really what you want. Either way, your life will work better, for you will no longer be dealing with illusion.

Carol:
Seminar Dialogue

"What if you just don't know what you want?" asked Carol. She was fortyish with short hair and an infectious grin. She was dressed in a bulky sweater and jeans.

"Well, what if, like Dorothy in *The Wizard of Oz,* you could click your heels together and have anything you wanted?" I asked.

"Anything?"

I nodded in reply. She thought for a long moment before answering. "I've always wanted to be a singer, but it's a little late for that."

"Not necessarily," I replied. "Can you sing?"

"Yes, I have a very good voice."

"Then how could you incorporate singing into your life?"

"It's impossible. I have to support myself and I couldn't go out on the road, like most bands do."

"Argue for your limitations and they shall be yours. Richard Bach wrote that," I said. "Never assume there is only one way to fulfill your desires. I know a lot of singers. My father-in-law sings in local opera productions. He works a regular job, but his after-work activities center around the opera group. That's where he finds his joy. Another friend of mine sings jingles and creates music for commercials. She started out part-time while holding down another job, but as the demand for her services grew, so did her income. Now singing is her full-time career. I'm sure there are hundreds of other approaches."

"I see," she said thoughtfully. "But do you really think you can do anything you want?"

"Yes, with three caveats: 1. As long as your goal doesn't manipulate another human being, 2. if you're willing to pay the price, and 3. your goal must be realistic. If you're sixty years old and have no background in politics, I doubt that you could become the President of the United States. If you're tone deaf, a career as a singer isn't realistic."

"I don't know that you're serving people by telling them things like this," she said. Her voice was resigned. "It could cause people to have foolish dreams."

"Is there such a thing as a foolish dream?" I asked.

Buckley:
Seminar Dialogue

"It's only now that I'm forty-eight years old, that my anger toward my father is beginning to come up," said Buckley, a balding man dressed in a conservative suit.

I nodded and waited.

Buckley continued. "My family wanted me to be educated as a lawyer and join the family banking business. I wanted to be a writer, but there was a lot of pressure from my father, and I finally complied. I was in banking for fifteen years before I started writing nonfiction books on the side. I've written eight in all, and they've sold well."

"You enjoy writing more than banking?" I asked.

"Yes, and I always did. Of course, I'm still in banking,

but if I had concentrated those years of my time and energy on writing, I know I could have been one of the best."

"Why the anger?"

"Because when I look back on how I was pressured to go into law and banking, I get very resentful of my father. I realize there is a lot of repressed stuff in here." He tapped his stomach.

"Could you express your resentment to your father?"

Buckley shook his head. "He's eighty-two years old. He wouldn't know what I was talking about. And I don't want to alienate him at this point in his life."

"A loss in the past is experienced as anger. Your loss is obvious—time to have established yourself in the field you loved best."

Buckley nodded.

"Why not write down everything you feel, with the idea that you'd like your father to read it. Take time, make sure every resentment, every emotion is covered. It might be fifty or a hundred pages. This will help you to pull up the emotions and purge them. Then, when it's all out and you've read and reread what you have written, burn it some ritualistic way, or go to the seashore and cast the pages into the waves."

Buckley smiled.

"Then forgive your father and let go of it and know that any further blame is nothing but self-pity."

"You're right," he said.

"And now, this is the first day of the rest of your life. Are you going to spend it writing or banking?"

Buckley laughed. His wife, sitting beside him, stood up and took the microphone. "It would mean some lifestyle changes for Buckley to make this career change, but I'm trying to talk him into doing it."

The participants applauded loudly.

Iris:
Seminar Dialogue

"My situation is a little different," Iris said. "I knew what I wanted to do, and I did it. Today, I think my parents are angry at me for enjoying my life." She was in her middle thirties, with short-cropped hair, wire-rimmed glasses, and casually dressed.

"Then that's what is, Iris. Most of the world isn't very self-actualized."

"But I can't help feeling guilty," she said. "I know it's silly, but I still feel guilty."

"For enjoying your life?"

"They certainly don't enjoy theirs."

"Does your guilt ever come out as anger toward your parents?" I asked.

She nodded. "Then I feel all the worse."

"Then you really question if you are deserving of your good life, don't you?"

"Yes."

"A common pattern is for you to invite more rejection from your parents, which helps you to feel punished."

"Yes, I guess so, but this is bullshit."

"I agree. You need to explore feelings that need to be expressed. How did it start?"

"I was clear in my intent to start my own business, but my parents told me it would fail and argued against it. They wanted me to keep working for the telephone company.

Anyway, I borrowed money, opened a bookstore, and it has been quite successful. The original debt has been repaid and I make double a phone company wage."

"You proved your parents wrong."

"Yes, I guess I did."

"Have you always enjoyed proving them wrong?" I asked.

"I don't know what you're talking about."

"Yes, you do, Iris."

She looked away, around the room and finally back at me. "Okay, so what? They've always been know-it-alls."

"It's your way of 'getting' your parents, and you feel guilty about your desire to get them. Do you like to shock them too?"

Iris scowled at me, hesitated, then said, "I guess so."

"They resisted you, probably way back when you were a young child, so you started resisting them. It became your relationship pattern—a love/hate situation."

Iris nodded and tears appeared in her eyes.

"The parental rejection resulted in anger, which you learned to hold inside. Because you loved your parents, you let it out in little, safe ways, right?"

"Right."

"Guilt created by numerous incidents over a long period of time results in rigid patterns of behavior. Some have actually served you. You probably succeeded in your business as much to prove your parents wrong as to prove yourself a success. You never really had clarity of intent, because you didn't start the business for the reasons you thought you did."

Iris laughed through her tears and nodded.

"Your relationship with your parents is the result of repressing your real feelings. Would you like the relationship to change, Iris?"

"Yes, I really would."

"Then what can *you* do to change it?"

"I guess I can start expressing my real feelings. I can accept mom and dad as they are without expecting them to change. I might as well, because I know they won't change."

"Anything else?"

She laughed. "Forgive them, right? And myself too."

"Sounds like a good place to start."

Chapter Fourteen
LACK OF ALIVENESS OR MOTIVATION

Aliveness is real enjoyment in doing what you do. It's the excitement and exhilaration that make you glad to be alive. It's the joy, stimulation, and pleasure that make life worth living. The best way I've found to generate aliveness and motivation is to get someone to do what they really want to do. What you want to do is always your best option in life, because life appears to be set up for you to get what you want—*if* you dare to want it. So, when you are making choices, choose what you want most, *not* which choice makes the most sense.

Action Required

To overcome lack of aliveness and motivate yourself, get involved in what really interests you. It is important to realize that you must have strength-producing activity in your life or you will become depressed. Your mind will never allow your life to become too boring and mundane without doing something to make it more interesting. The problem is, it might generate fights with your mate (when you're in mental pain, at least you know you're alive), or an illness (kidney stones would give you something to talk about), or an accident (endangering your life will create a lot of aliveness). The idea is to make life interesting before your mind does it for you.

Jeff:
Seminar Dialogue

"Decide what really motivates you, and just do it," Jeff said. He was in his early thirties and dressed in Levi's and a sweater. "But what if there just isn't anything that gets your juices flowing? I'd love to be really excited about a direction." He turned and looked at the other seminar participants. "But I'm not." Many of the other participants nodded in agreement.

"Nothing in life excites you?" I asked.

He looked at me for a moment, then said, "Sex. Do you think I should be a male prostitute?"

"Would it create aliveness?"

He shook his head. "Deadness, probably, the AIDS situation being what it is."

"Nothing else excites you?"

"Basketball, but I'm too old and too short."

"With the exception of sex and basketball, life is just a drag?"

He didn't reply.

"What do you think you'll be doing five years from now, Jeff?"

"Probably the same thing I'm doing now. Working as an assistant manager in a grocery store."

"Ten years from now?"

"I might make it to manager. Whoopie do!"

"If you could generate the motivation, what would you consider doing?"

"Acting."

"This is the town for it."

"It takes a lot of hard work and self-discipline. There's intense competition. I don't like dealing with difficulties."

"Why are you attending this seminar, Jeff?"

"In hope of finding magical answers." He flashed a silly smile.

"What have you found so far?"

"That you have to decide what you want, blast through the blocks, and pay a price to get it."

I laughed.

Jeff continued. "An astrologer told me I have a bland chart."

"Astrology doesn't block free will, Jeff. But, maybe you'll just have to make it all right with yourself to be the person you are, rather than who you can be."

He shook his head.

"Jeff, there are no magic answers. If you can't sort through life's unlimited potentials and find something that interests you, then your life is never going to change. No one else can do it for you. Certainly, you can understand that?"

"A lot of other people in this seminar don't feel any motivation either," Jeff said.

"And nowhere is it written that you should," I added. "My point is only that aliveness results from doing what you

127

love to do. Life seems to be set up for you to get what you want, *if* you dare to want it."

"I'm going to keep thinking about it," Jeff said, sitting down.

Marina:
Seminar Dialogue

"Even if I was Dorothy in *The Wizard of Oz*, and could click my heels together and have anything I wanted, I wouldn't know what to wish for," Marina said, raising her hands in a gesture of futility. She was dressed in designer casual wear and wore a wistful expression on her face.

"You're not alone, Marina. How many people in this room are willing to admit that they really don't know exactly what they want out of life? Be straight!" I raised my hand, indicating I wanted them to raise theirs if they were not clear on their intent. Half the hands in the ballroom of three hundred people were raised.

Marina looked around. She shrugged her shoulders and said, "That doesn't make me feel any better."

"All right, Marina, I would suggest that you and everyone who just raised their hand put first things first. Make it a priority to discover what would generate happiness and fulfillment for you. Happiness and fulfillment come from within, not from another person. Someone else can add to your happiness but they can't make you happy. It's time to dream your dreams. It's time to ask yourself, 'What do I really enjoy doing? What do I do naturally and well?'

"Consider doing only what you enjoy in life. If you don't enjoy it, don't do it—delegate it to someone who does enjoy it. You may have to work a little longer at what you *do* enjoy

128

to earn the money to hire someone to do what you *don't* enjoy. But that's fine, do it. Some of you are saying to yourself, 'how silly, how stupid.' If so, you're arguing for your limitations and reducing your options. And if you do that in this training room with me, you do it in the rest of your life.

"We're here on earth to learn to let go of fear and express unconditional love. As part of the process we learn that life is what we make it. And hopefully we learn the most important lesson of all."

I slowly scanned the room, making eye contact with as many people as possible. "LIFE IS TO BE ENJOYED!"

 *"I end up saying 'screw it all,' and just kick back and watch TV."*

Chapter Fifteen

LACK OF
SELF-DISCIPLINE

Self-discipline is the basis of all self-change. It isn't about self-denial or self-restriction. In the context of success it means self-determination. Perseverance in action is the very basis of success because it is how you direct your time, energy and resources to manifest your desires. Self-discipline is the one factor common to all self-made, successful people. Simply said, it means you do what you need to do when you need to do it and stop doing what doesn't work.

Action Required

If you are confused about goals and values and you lack clarity of intent, you will also lack self-discipline. So first, re-evaluate those factors. Lack of self-discipline also manifests in procrastination, avoiding or indefinitely postponing chores or projects you dislike doing. If there is no way around what needs to be done, and you can't delegate the work to someone else, then you must accept "what is" and handle it. Large projects can be especially overpowering, but good planning can help you to get going. Direct your time and energy to maximize your efforts and do the job one step at a time until it's done. Remind yourself that you are doing the job because you freely choose to do it, not because you are being forced to. (In reality, you don't have to do anything.) It may also help to begin controlling the negative thoughts influencing your actions.

Jack:
Seminar Dialogue

"It's easy for you to say 'handle it,' but it's a hell of a lot harder to do it," Jack said. He was a bald, overweight man in his early forties, dressed in tan slacks and sport shirt.

"What exactly are we talking about, Jack?" I asked.

"Everything. Handle the right diet, handle the household chores, improve my business, search for spiritual meaning, deal with my father's needs, and my wife's needs, and my kid's needs. I end up saying 'screw it all,' and just kick back and watch TV."

"What do you do for a living?"

"I own a retail jewelry store."

"Is it stressful?"

"Very. I deal with rich bitches all day long."

"You don't tell your customers what you really think?"

"Of course not. They'd walk out of the store in a huff."

"So you repress your emotions all day, which generates stress, then at night you watch TV to release the stress. Research shows that two-thirds of the time while watching TV, most people are in an altered state of consciousness.

That means your brain is releasing beta-endorphins and other internally manufactured opiates into your system to calm you down. The problem is, TV viewing also drains you, leaving you with little energy for anything else."

Jack looked at me without responding so I asked, "How much TV do you watch?"

"From about 7 P.M. through the news and usually the *Tonight Show*."

"That's five and a half hours a night. You could certainly do a lot with five and a half extra hours a day, couldn't you?" He shrugged. "You could get the same brain-opiate release by running, doing meditation, or using hypnosis tapes. But in these cases, rather than being drained, you'd be revitalized."

"It's too much work."

"Using a hypnosis tape is too much work?"

"Making myself do it."

"You make yourself sit down and turn on the TV set. Instead, make yourself lie down and turn on a hypnosis tape."

"It would calm me down?"

I nodded. "How's your sex life, Jack?"

"What?"

"How often do you have sex with your wife?"

"Once every week or so, why?"

"Is she happy with that?"

"I guess so. We're both so tired by the time we go to bed."

"Because you've been drained by five and a half hours of television. I'll bet you drink diet cola to fight the energy drain while you watch TV. The sweetener and caffeine in these drinks perk you up, then drop you down and generate anger." This fact seemed to get Jack's attention.

"Is that for real? My wife and I often get snitty at each other as the evening goes on. But I thought it was just because we don't necessarily like the same shows."

I shrugged. "Jack, if you want to be more self-disciplined, you have to make the time available to do what needs to be done. You're watching over thirty-eight hours of television a week, which is just about all your extra time. How about getting a life? The only benefit of TV viewing is mind-numbing escape, which you can obtain other ways. Decide on your priorities, map out a one-step-at-a-time plan, and get at it."

"Diet cola, huh?"

I shook my head. Jack sat down.

Linda Sue:
Seminar Dialogue

Linda Sue was a radiant woman in her middle thirties whose voice alone projected aliveness. I had noticed how the other seminar participants were attracted to her positive energy, and how they gathered around her at the bathroom breaks. Holding the microphone, she said, "I want to start my own business, but I seem to lack the self-discipline to take the steps necessary to set things into motion."

"What steps?" I asked.

"I'd like to start a flower shop. There's none in the area where I live. But I need to find financing, a location, suppliers, and all the necessary backup services, such as an accountant and an association with wire services."

"Do you really know the flower shop business?"

She shook her head. "No, but I love flowers." She laughed. "I currently work in a dress shop, but maybe I should get a job in a flower shop to learn the business?''

I waited.

"That's a good idea. Then it probably won't seem so overwhelming," she said.

Laughing, I said, "And when it's time to act, maybe you can delegate the overwhelming aspects of launching the business. Use professionals to help find the rest of the answers."

Linda Sue sat down. I continued. "You need to understand exactly what you're dealing with to clarify your goals. Then you can map out a plan of workable steps."

Adora:
Seminar Dialogue

"I drink coffee, smoke cigarettes and eat candy to give myself the energy to fulfill my goals," Adora said, gesturing with the microphone. She brushed her free hand through her graying hair and smiled at me.

I shook my head. "Coffee, cigarettes and candy, which lift you up and drop you down, necessitating more of the same."

She nodded. "But I sure get a lot done."

"Until your body collapses."

"It's holding together pretty good." She giggled and tossed her shoulders back.

"Tell me about your goals," I said.

"To read two books a week, work on a book I'm writing, keep up my correspondence, do my exercise, talk to my friends ... everything."

"Forgetting for a moment that you are addicted to caffeine, nicotine and sugar, what would happen if you were to live your life without these stimulants?"

"It would be the end of my self-discipline. I'd become a couch potato."

"I don't think so. Proper nutrition could supply you with high energy without destroying your body. But let's look at this from another angle. Let's explore your priorities. You have a lot you want to do and you have only so many extra hours in a day. What is most important?"

"Exercise keeps me sane, and I really want to finish my book. It's a mystery and a writer friend says it's good."

"How many hours a day?"

"Two or three."

"What could you drop from your schedule?"

"I could read one book every two weeks and it wouldn't really change my life. Books are my TV. My phone time is usually nothing but negative gossip. Actually, I'd like an excuse to end a lot of it. My correspondence? I could probably cut it in half and the people I write to would be relieved." She shook her head and smiled. "I wouldn't need as much energy would I? But I love coffee, cigarettes and candy."

I looked at her without responding.

"Give up the goodies," she said, nodding and sitting down.

I scanned the group of participants. "What do you really want to do? If you're excited about it, you'll find the self-discipline to do it. You need to be clear on your intent—the clearer the better. Also, it's a lot easier to find the self-discipline for an emotional goal than it is for a practical goal. The book Adora is writing is an emotional goal that will result in great ego satisfaction."

Charles:
Seminar Dialogue

"I don't understand what you mean by controlling your thoughts as a way to increase self-discipline," Charles said. He was in his late thirties and dressed in a casual cotton suit and a white silk shirt worn buttoned at the top with no tie.

"If you could generate more self-discipline, how would you use it?" I asked.

"Probably to develop my tennis game."

"What keeps you from developing your tennis game?"

"I play with friends of equal ability, which is fun, but I don't seem to be getting any better. I could be taking lessons and practicing more with the ball machine. But I don't think I have the hand-eye coordination to get much better."

"That last thought doesn't serve you, Charles. From now on, every time you think that, catch yourself and say, 'success opportunity.' Then rephrase the thought, something to the effect of, 'I have the ability to be a great tennis player.'"

"Got it. Thanks."

Directing my words to the participants, I said, "Remember, your mind operates like a computer and your thoughts are your programming software. It's a good idea to reverse the power of every negative thought, including those relating to self-discipline. If you say, 'I'd love to do that, but I don't have the energy.' Catch yourself, say 'success opportunity,' and reverse the thought's power by reframing the words. 'I'd love to do that, and I have incredible energy to do it.' Do it even if you don't have the energy, because the positive programming will help to give you the energy."

Chapter Sixteen
MISPLACED PASSION

Misplaced passion is a matter of having great energy and enthusiasm for something that doesn't serve you or offers little potential for success. Example: You love motorcycles more than anything in the world. You read everything ever written about motorcycles, spend your evenings and weekends riding motorcycles, and any remaining spare time is spent talking with friends about motorcycles. At the same time you have little or no energy for your business, a small travel agency. You know if you were to spend some of your energy investigating unique travel aspects and promoting them to potential customers, your business would improve. But you don't do it.

Action Required

First, explore the emotional needs your misplaced passion is fulfilling. In the motorcycle situation, it might be the sense of freedom you experience on the bike, or the satisfaction to be found in tinkering with a precise mechanical object. This being the case, there might be ways to fulfill these needs as a part of your travel business.

Ideally, by following your passion you can parlay your passionate energy into success. Maybe in the above case, you'd be better off selling your travel agency and opening a motorcycle shop. If there are already too many motorcycle shops in your town, you might have to move to another town. If that isn't a viable option, you'll have to accept the success level of your travel agency while knowing you have the potential to improve it. Or you might try to integrate your business and passion by creating motorcycle safaris, or arranging European motorcycle vacations. If this isn't possible and your business demands more attention, you'll have to find the self-discipline to sacrifice some of the time you spend on your motorcycle and apply it to your business instead.

Danny:
Seminar Dialogue

"My misplaced passion is for cowboy bars," Danny said. "And here in Phoenix there are plenty of them." In his late twenties, he sported a pearl-button Western shirt, jeans and boots.

"Can you explain a little more?" I asked.

"Sure. I enjoy all the excitement. Sometimes I get beat up and I don't like that. My wife hates it, and it's a source of trouble in our marriage. Especially since I was ticketed for drunk driving."

"Okay, Danny. What do you get out of going to the bars? First, excitement; second, time with your buddies; third, escape from day-to-day reality. Anything else?"

"Country music."

"All right, that's four things. How could you obtain excitement, comradeship, escape, and music, without going to country bars?"

"Lots of ways."

"Then it would be easy for you to give up your misplaced passion and replace it with positive passions that would serve your marriage. Maybe some activities you could enjoy with your wife."

Addressing myself to the group, I said, "If you know what you're doing isn't working, ask yourself what emotional needs you are satisfying by doing what you do. Chances are there is more than one way to satisfy those needs."

Shelly:
Seminar Dialogue

"But my misplaced passion is for skydiving," Shelly said. "It's expensive, dangerous, and it makes my boyfriend crazy. But I can't seem to stop." She was probably about thirty, pretty, with long, raven hair. She was dressed in the latest West Hollywood fashion.

"Tell me how you got started," I said.

"I was dating a skydiver. He talked me into trying it. Now he's out of the picture and I date a musician who has no interest in diving out of an airplane."

"You were scared to death the first time you jumped, right?"

"Right."

"What you're experiencing is the natural result of your actions. If you fear doing something and have the courage to do it anyway, your mind will often perform a flip-flop and you may even become addicted to doing it. Why? Because the excitement of the experience generates the release of brain/mind opiates—chemicals resembling opium and quite addictive. The more you skydive, the more you want to skydive. This applies to any exciting, internally stimulating experience, such as downhill skiing, risky business ventures, sexual affairs, public speaking, meeting new people, or whatever you originally feared."

"But what can I do about it?"

"The same chemicals are released in meditation, hypnosis, running, or any other activity that generates an altered state of consciousness. Your boyfriend may go into an altered state when he plays his music. I do when I sit at my computer writing a book or magazine article. Writing is quite addictive."

"My boyfriend will be glad I asked," she said.

Adrian:
Seminar Dialogue

"Metaphysics is my misplaced passion, according to my husband," Adrian said. "He hates anything to do with New Age ideas or awareness." She was an attractive middle-aged woman wearing a long dress that reminded me of Haight-Ashbury in the sixties. She turned toward the audience as she spoke and I noticed many other women nodding their heads in agreement. As in most seminars, eighty percent of the participants were women.

"He wants you to be interested in what he wants you to be interested in?" I said.

"That's about it," she said laughing.

"Want to explore it?"

"This whole seminar has been about exploring it," she said and sighed. "And he'd better get used to it."

Chapter Seventeen

KARMA, REINCARNATION & HIGHER SELF

You now have an awareness of the Critical 15 factors that create turmoil in the lives of human beings. To resolve your own conflicts, all you have to do is recognize the factors affecting you, then act to correct the problem! Easier said than done? Of course, but you can't change what you don't recognize. Recognizing the problem for what it *really* is, is the first step to resolving it. You may want to further explore the cause of your beliefs and attitudes with regressive hypnosis—either on your own, with a regressive hypnotist, or using prerecorded hypnosis tapes, such as those described in the back of this book.

Karma & Reincarnation

Reincarnation and karma play an important part in the

explanations and dialogues in this volume. If you've read my other books, you can skip this chapter. If you don't have an understanding of karma, this awareness will help you to fully understand the concepts.

I contend that this is either a random universe or there is some kind of plan. By random universe, I mean that we evolved over the centuries to our present state, and when we die, we become nothing. If this is so, life is meaningless. But if there is a plan, then it would follow that there is an intelligence behind the plan. You can call this intelligence George, Ginger, God, universal mind, an energy gestalt, the collective unconscious, or any other name that works for you.

And if there is a plan, wouldn't it also follow that justice would be part of the plan? Justice! But look around you. Where is the justification for all the misery and inequality in the world? How can you justify child abuse, mass starvation, rapes, murders, wars, victims of violence, people ripping off others and seemingly being rewarded for it?

Karma can explain it all. I've studied philosophy and religion all my adult life and nothing else can logically explain the inequality. Karma rewards and punishes. It is a multi-life debit and credit system that offers total justice. But don't forget that karma either is or it isn't. There can be no halfway plan, no halfway justice. Either absolutely everything is karmic or nothing is karmic. You need to accept or reject the concept of karma; it is senseless and confusing to accept a halfway position.

Now, to bring some of this awareness together, if I pick up a stone and toss it into a pond, I am the cause and the effect is the splash and ripples. I have disturbed the harmony of the pond. The ripples flow out and back until, due to the physical law of dissipation of energy, the pond eventually returns to its original harmonious state.

Like the ripples, your thoughts, words and actions create vibrations that flow out into the universe and back to you until eventually, over many lifetimes, you balance your karma and your harmony is restored. Everything you **think, say** and **do** creates or erases karma. And, as if that's not enough to deal with, this includes the **motive, intent** and **desire** behind every thought, word and action.

When you begin to explore the motive, intent and desire behind everything you think, say and do, you'll find you're asking yourself a lot of questions. Are you helping your friend out of true compassion or because it pumps your ego? Or because your friend is now in debt to you? Do you give to charity at the office because you desire to help, or because you are afraid of what people in the office will think if you don't? It's easy to look like you're creating harmonious karma when you really aren't, because your motive, intent or desire are not what they appear to be. *Why* you do what you do is just as important as *what* you do from a karmic perspective.

I also contend that neither God nor the Lords of Karma bestow your suffering upon you. It is *your* decision and *yours alone* to either accept or refuse to deal with the opportunities you are experiencing in your life. *You* are responsible for absolutely everything that has ever happened to you. You are your own judge and jury. On a Higher-Self level of awareness, you are aware that in order to progress, you must learn. And the fastest way to learn is by directly experiencing the consequences of your own actions.

If you and you alone are responsible for everything that has ever happened to you, that means there is no one to blame for *anything* that has ever happened to you. **There is no one to blame for anything!** The concept of blame is totally incompatible with karma. There are no victims. The ex-mate you had such a hard time with, the partner who ripped you off, the in-laws you hated, your sadistic boss, the guy who raped you when you were twelve, the burglars who robbed your house ... you created them all because you needed the balance and the test.

Take a moment and think back on your life. Think about everyone in your past who really made life difficult for you. In actuality, these were the people who helped you the most in accomplishing your goal of spiritual evolution. They helped you balance your karma. They were a test you created to determine how you're progressing.

It is easy to tell whether you are passing or failing your own tests. If you respond with love, positive thoughts, compassion, or even neutrality, and can fully let go of the past, you are probably passing the test. If you respond with negativity, blame, or desire for revenge, you are probably failing the test. And if you choose to fail, that's all right ... you'll just have to come back and try it again, probably with the same person. If one person learns and the other doesn't, the one who didn't learn will connect with someone who has similar karmic configurations, and they will come together to test themselves in the future.

Often in balancing karma, you don't even have to wait for the next lifetime for an opportunity to arise. We have all observed recurring, undesirable patterns in others, as well as in ourselves. This is a situation of learning through *pain* until we finally "get it," once and for all, that what we are doing doesn't work.

You were born with a package of karma that you desired to experience. From a spiritual perspective, if you are testing yourself, it is only your reactions to the experiences that are important.

When we are on the other side in spirit, preparing to enter into a lifetime, we seem to be very brave. For instance, you may say to yourself, "Okay, I think I'm ready to test myself in another relationship with Donald. If he's willing, we'll fall in love, get married and have three children. When I'm about thirty-two, Donald will begin to ignore me and start having affairs with other women. This time, because I owe Don one in this area, I'll emotionally support him and let him go with unconditional love."

As I said, you are brave and aware over there on the other side. Now comes the reality. And what do you do? You scream and threaten and blame. You hire a lawyer who socks it to Donald financially for the rest of his days. You and Donald now hate each other. This is another example of learning through pain. You and Don can plan to return for another round in the year 2046; maybe next time you'll work it out.

Actually, there is no such thing as failing your own karmic test. If you fell off your bicycle nine times before you finally learned to ride, the nine failures were actually small successes which eventually led to the ultimate success. How many times you fail before reaching your goal is up to you.

In addition to your birth karma, you create new karma every day, harmonious and disharmonious. And you pay it off every day through the balancing effects of your subconscious mind. There is also karma as yet unknown to you. It is stored up from the past, awaiting a suitable opportunity to discharge itself. This could happen later in this life or in your next life or the lifetime after that. Not everything can be balanced in one lifetime.

But the good news is, **the Law of Grace supersedes the Law of Karma.** This means that if you give love, grace and mercy, you will receive it in return. All of your positive, loving thoughts and actions go to cancel your stored-up bad karma. Since this is so, it is probably time for you to begin thinking how you can be more positive, loving and compassionate; how you can support good works and serve this planet ... if only to reduce the amount of undesirable karma that you have waiting for you in your future.

I also contend that **wisdom erases karma** and that we can mitigate karmic discomforts through awareness. The techniques of past-life therapy are often of value in this area. In the past, we've learned through pain. In other words, we've learned not to touch hot stoves because by touching hot stoves, we burn our fingers. After experiencing the pain of a few burnt fingers, we finally learn, once and for all, that this is a bad idea. Karmic lessons are the hot stoves we need to learn from in life.

To learn through wisdom, you must forgive yourself. Since you are your own judge and jury, it is up to you to forgive yourself. The only problem is that you will not do this unless, on the level of Higher Mind, you know the karma is totally balanced or that the lesson is learned. You can't fool yourself in this area. To truly forgive yourself, you must know, on every level of your body and mind, that you will never, ever forget the lesson again. Of course, to release the karma, you must also be able to sincerely forgive all the others involved.

If you are not yet able to forgive to this degree, and you are determined to rise above the karmic effect, you must decide what you can do to achieve this desired level of self-forgiveness. Can you do something symbolic to show that you have learned? Can you assist others as a form of restitution?

Through working with people in past-life therapy, I've found that a technique I call "symbolic restitution" can be very helpful. As an example, a woman named Susan wanted but could not have a baby. She and her husband consulted doctors and subjected themselves to every kind of fertility test. In the end, the tests showed that there was no physical reason the woman could not conceive. "It must be a mental block," her doctor explained, suggesting she see a psychiatrist.

Instead, Susan explored a "back to the cause" hypnotic regression and re-experienced abandoning a baby in 18th Century England. Instead of making sure the child was cared for, the Englishwoman left it in the woods to die. In the Higher-Self portion of the session, she was told, "You must learn the value of life, what a blessing it is to have a child … and about the responsibility of being a parent. Until you know these things you will not trust yourself to birth another."

As a form of symbolic restitution, Susan became a volunteer in a Shriner's Hospital for crippled children. The last time I talked to her she said, "I see the parents in agony over what their children are going through. I cry over the little ones when they return from the operating room. I have such a different perspective now."

I'll bet one day soon I'll receive a birth announcement from Susan.

In summary, knowledge of past lives can help us to better understand that which influences, restricts or motivates us in the present. Sometimes, in cases of false-fear karma and false-guilt karma, just knowing the cause of the problem resolves the effect.

The Five Kinds of Karma

Based upon nearly twenty years of directing past-life regressions, I've found I can fit any kind of karma into one of five basic categories. Sometimes this situation will cover two of these categories at one time. As an example, balancing karma might also be reward karma. Physical karma might also be balancing karma.

Balancing Karma

This is the most simplistic, mechanical kind of cause and effect. Examples of balancing karma would be a lonely man who seeks unsuccessfully to establish a relationship. In a past life, he used others so cruelly that he needs to learn the value of a relationship.

Other examples: A man who is always overlooked for promotion because in a past life he destroyed others to attain wealth and power; a woman who suffers continual, severe migraine headaches because, in a fit of jealousy, she hit her lover on the head and killed him in a past life; a man who is born blind because, as a Roman soldier, he purposely blinded Christian prisoners.

Physical Karma

Physical karma is a situation in which a past-life problem or misuse of the body results in an appropriate affliction in a later life. Physical karma often results from reincarnating too soon—before the etheric body has reformed.

As an example, a man with pneumonia had his lungs drained through a tube and was left with a deeply indented scar under his left arm. Upon dying, he remained on the other side only a short time before being reborn as a female with a blood sack under her left arm. Examining the baby, the doctor said, "There's a hole there. If it doesn't close on its own, we'll have to go in and sew it up."

Other examples: A child born with lung problems might have died from lung cancer due to excessive smoking in a past life. Another man had a disfiguring birthmark that was a carry-over from a terrible burn in another incarnation.

False-Fear Karma

False-fear karma is created when a traumatic past-life incident generates a fear that is not valid in the context of the current life.

For example, a workaholic discovered during regression that he was unable to feed his family during a time of famine in the Middle Ages. In his past-life regression, he re-experienced the pain of burying a child who starved to death. In his current life, his subconscious mind is attempting to avert any potential duplication of that terrible pain, thus generating an internal drive to work day and night to assure adequate provisions for his family in this incarnation.

False-fear karma and false-guilt karma are the easiest to

resolve through past-life therapy techniques because once the individuals understand the origin of the fear and/or guilt, they can see how it no longer applies to them in their current lifetime.

False-Guilt Karma

False-guilt karma occurs when an individual takes on the responsibility or accepts the blame for a traumatic past-life incident for which he or she is blameless.

A man who contracted polio resulting in a paralyzed leg perceived as the past-life cause his being the driver of a car which was involved in an accident that crippled a child. Although it wasn't his fault, he blamed himself and sought self-forgiveness through this karmic affliction.

Continuing problems involving depression, pain, and/or emotional trauma can usually be traced back to a past tragedy of some kind in which guilt is associated with the event. This can be false guilt or a situation in which the troubled individual was actually responsible for the tragedy.

Developed Ability & Awareness Karma (Reward Karma)

Abilities and awareness are developed over a period of many lifetimes.

As examples, a man in Rome became interested in music and began to develop his ability. Today, after six additional lifetimes in which he refined his ability during each incarnation, he is a successful professional musician. A woman happily married for thirty-five years has worked hard to refine her awareness of human relationships over many lifetimes.

The abilities and awareness that you master over a period of lifetimes are yours to keep forever, although they may lie latent, buried deep within you, waiting for a time when it is appropriate to call them into your present existence.

HIGHER SELF

There are three mind levels: The conscious, the subconscious and the superconscious, which is also called Higher Self.

Conscious Mind: Will, reason, logic, and the five physical senses.

Subconscious Mind: The memory banks, containing all your past programming, including beliefs, habit patterns, emotional programming and the Akashic records of all the lifetimes you have ever lived.

Superconscious Mind (Higher Self): The creative force and psychic abilities, the collective awareness of mankind, plus unlimited, unknown powers. When you attain a Higher-Self level of consciousness, you have at your mental fingertips an awareness of your totality, and the collective totality of the energy gestalt we can call "God." We are all part of the collective unconscious—the greater body of mankind—thus we are all "one."

Going back to my book, *You Were Born Again To Be Together* (1976, Pocket Books), I wrote about Higher Self:

The superconscious mind is often referred to metaphysically as the Higher Self—the God self or the I AM. It is the power behind creative and psychic abilities. It is also unlimited in power and wisdom. Every man has consummate genius within him. By opening the doors to the superconscious, you can do anything as long as you use the power in

DICK SUTPHEN

a positive way. Thus you have the ability to self-bestow your own happiness and success, or to achieve help and guidance beyond anything we can consciously imagine.

Within this Higher-Self level there is a larger, universal perspective of which we must be aware when seeking the truth. We judge from an earthbound perspective, based on logic, sequential time, and science. Earthbound perspective would claim heredity and environment determine our lives. Universal perspective would teach that you choose your parents, environment, and time and place of birth for the experience and opportunities they offer ... and that your present-life circumstances were determined by your past lives and your current-incarnation programming.

If we could truly know ourselves—our *Higher Selves*— we would live in a world of cooperation, love, and wisdom.

 *It really amounts to knowing your goal, concentrating on it, remaining determined and having the self-discipline to complete what you are doing.*

Chapter Eighteen
WHAT MAKES PEOPLE HAPPY?

What else can you do to create the life you want to live? You can learn to "flow", according to Mihaly Csikszentmihalyi. In his book, *FLOW—The Psychology of Optimal Experience* (Harper Perennial), Csikszentmihalyi says, "More than anything else, people seek happiness." The author is a professor and former chairman of the Department of Psychology at the University of Chicago. He has spent twenty years researching topics related to this psychology of optimal experience, research that has now taken on worldwide interest.

Happiness is sought for its own sake, but all our other goals—health, beauty, money or power—are valued because we expect that they will make us happy. Csikszentmihalyi began his happiness research by studying hundreds of "experts"—artists, athletes, musicians, chess masters, and surgeons—in other words, people who spend their time doing the activities they prefer. From their accounts he developed a theory of optimal experience based on what he calls flow—"the state in which people are so involved in an activity that nothing else seems to matter; the experience itself is so enjoyable that people will do it even at great cost, for the sheer sake of doing it."

Further research indicated that flow wasn't limited to "experts." Men and women, rich and poor, young and old, regardless of culture, can experience flow. The flow research included old women in Korea, adults in Thailand and India, teenagers in Tokyo, Navajo sheepherders, and people working on assembly lines in Chicago. And the research concludes that the happiest people spend much time in a state of flow.

In exploring Csikszentmihalyi's research, it became obvious to me that the common factor in flow is a natural altered state of consciousness. He claims flow is addictive. As I've explained in previous chapters, being in an altered state is addictive because the brain releases soothing opiates into the central nervous system. And an eyes-open altered state is a matter of focusing your attention on one thing, which is the key factor in flow.

Although Csikszentmihalyi doesn't mention altered states, his work shows that when psychic energy (attention) is invested in realistic goals and when your skills match the opportunities for action, flow results. The pursuit of your goals brings such intense concentration that you momentarily forget everything else. In so doing you achieve control over your psychic energy, and by stretching skills and reaching toward higher challenges, you become an increasingly extraordinary individual.

The research clearly states that people who regularly experience flow are stronger people who can more easily handle life's ups and downs without caving in. To fully enjoy your life, learn to transform your activities into flow.

As a writer, I'm in flow most of the day. The same is true if I'm reading or playing tennis. Mihaly often mentions tennis as a flow activity because of the need for intense concentration and to monitor feedback.

The rules of how to achieve flow are easy enough and within everyone's reach. So why don't more people experience this positive state of mind? Because there are many forces, internal and external, that stand in the way. It's a little like losing weight. Those interested in losing weight know what it takes. But as much as they want to lose weight, it's extremely difficult for many. The stakes here are higher. It's not a matter of losing a few extra pounds, it's a matter of losing a chance to improve the quality of your life.

The majority of people diffuse their attention in hundreds of random ways. Those who flow focus their attention intentionally upon the task at hand. It really amounts to knowing your goal, concentrating on it, remaining determined and having the self-discipline to complete what you are doing.

You create yourself by how you invest your energy. When it's under control your attention is focused. Attention is your most important tool in the task of improving the quality of your experience.

Flow Factors

1. Choose a task that you have a good chance of completing.

2. You need the ability to focus your concentration upon the task at hand. (Hypnosis programming tapes will help.)

3. Clear goals are necessary, allowing you to focus your concentration.

4. The task provides feedback, which allows you to focus your concentration.

5. You get so involved in the task that you forget about everything else.

6. The task allows you to exercise a sense of control over your actions.

7. You become so focused on the task that self-concern disappears. (Your sense of self returns, stronger than ever, after the flow experience is completed.)

8. You lose your sense of time; hours seem to pass in minutes, minutes can stretch out and seem like hours.

The combination of these factors causes a sense of deep enjoyment that is intensely gratifying. With this knowledge, it's possible to achieve control of consciousness and turn even routine tasks into an experience of flow.

Remember, flow is when all your relevant skills are needed to cope with the challenges of a task, and you become completely absorbed by the activity. No attention is left to process any information but what the activity offers. All your attention is focused on the various aspects of the task.

A person who is healthy, rich, strong, and powerful has no greater odds of being in control of his consciousness than one who is sickly, poor and oppressed.

Those who naturally experience flow appear to have an "autotelic" self. The word is made up of two Greek words meaning "self goal." Most people have goals that are shaped by biological needs and social conventions. In other words, the goals are generated externally. Those with an autotelic self have self-contained goals, and they accept few if any goals from outside themselves. They aren't bored, seldom experience anxiety, and easily translate threats into challenges, thus maintaining inner harmony.

To become an autotelic "flow" personality you need to set clear goals and learn to make decisions with a minimum of anxiety. Then you must be responsible to the challenges by developing the skills necessary to accomplish the goals. This means you'll have to learn to monitor feedback and incorporate constantly updated awareness into the project.

You must also become deeply involved in your task—balancing opportunities for action with the skills you possess. Your expectations must be halfway realistic, and your goals must challenge you.

Another important aspect of an autotelic self is the development of the self-discipline necessary to sustain your involvement until you accomplish your goal. Finally, you must learn to enjoy the immediate experience—live in the now while working for the accomplishment of the goal in the future.

Once you are flowing, the experience drives you on to more creativity and achievement. The development of increasingly refined skills to sustain enjoyment is the actual power behind the evolution of culture.

If this short synopsis of the flow experience is intriguing to you, I suggest you read Csikszentmihalyi's book.

164

Chapter Nineteen

REINVENTING
YOURSELF

In addition to recognizing needed changes, removing blocks, establishing goals, and incorporating the happiness potential of an autotelic personality, it's important to become aware of the qualities of the people who make the time and exert the effort to actually reinvent themselves.

1. Although you must find joy and fulfillment in the present, your peace of mind, health, survival, and success depend upon your willingness to commit to the future. Regularly remind yourself why you are doing what you're doing, and visualize your goals as if they were already accomplished.

2. Commit yourself to values and purpose. Those who reinvent themselves set priorities and are always achieving productively. They know that you must have goals if you want to grow, so they organize their time around the things that matter to them.

3. You need quiet time alone for introspection, to explore potentials, and to nurture yourself. Schedule regular times to withdraw and listen to your inner voice.

4. To pursue your best options, you must be adaptive to change. Be open to new perspectives, altered goals and new ways of thinking. Distinguish between what is and isn't essential, what will endure from what is temporary.

5. Learn from your stress, failures, misfortunes, conflicts, and disagreements. Discovering what doesn't work can help you to learn what does work. Look for the gift in your problems, view the problems as opportunities, and be confident in the future.

6. Pace yourself. You need more than occasional breaks in routine to reinvent yourself. Make time for travel, vacations, seminars, exercise, vigorous activities, and sabbaticals. Everyone has the same number of hours in the day; we either spend it or waste it. Spending it means to pass time in a specific way. Wasting it means just that. Sometimes the best way to spend time is to do nothing.

7. Always continue to study and learn, remaining focused upon who and what you are becoming.

8. Take the initiative to sustain your relationships with your mate, family and friends. Network information, contacts and resources.

9. Be concerned with quality, not just quantity.

10. Never remain on a comfortable plateau for very long. Continual challenge is important to maintain happiness and self-esteem.

11. Look internally for your motivation. People tend to be motivated externally or internally. The externally motivated find their enjoyment through contact with friends, acquiring

possessions, doing something to improve their physical appearance, and from pleasurable events such as parties, sports events, movies, and concerts. This momentary pleasure is usually only relief from boredom. Internally motivated people find fulfillment in creating, learning and accomplishing, all of which increase self-esteem.

12. Always act in ways that support your self-esteem, because you can only attract into your life what you feel worthy of. Every day, remind yourself that you are worthy and deserving of the very best that life has to offer.

* * * * *

As I said in the opening sentence of this book. *"How* to reinvent yourself is easy."* Now all you have to do is decide *who* you want to become, and do it.

About The Author

Dick Sutphen is the author of fourteen metaphysical books, seven for Simon & Schuster Pocket Books, including the bestselling **You Were Born Again To Be Together**. Recent titles include **Predestined Love, Finding Your Answers Within, Earthly Purpose,** and **The Oracle Within.**

Over 100,000 people have attended a Sutphen Seminar, which are conducted in major cities throughout the country. Sutphen has created a line of over 350 audio and video mind-programming tapes and publishes a major line of New Age music. He lives with his wife Tara and their children in Malibu, California.

FREE SUBSCRIPTION
(Just Send Us Your Receipt For This Book)

Dick Sutphen publishes *Master of Life WINNERS,* a quarterly magazine sent FREE to all Valley of the Sun book/tape buyers and seminar attendees. We'll be glad to mail you a free sample issue, or if you'll send us your receipt for this book, we'll send the magazine free for a year. Each issue is approximately 100 pages and contains news, research reports and articles on the subjects of metaphysics, psychic exploration and self-help, in addition to information on all Sutphen Seminars, and over 350 audio and video tapes: hypnosis, meditation, sleep programming, subliminal programming, silent subliminals, and New Age music. A sampling of some of our audio and video tapes that relate to the content of **Reinventing Yourself** will be found on the following pages.

Valley of the Sun Publishing
Box 3004, Agoura Hills, CA 91376
Phone: 818/889-1575

Audio/Video Tapes That Relate To This Book
Available Through Your Local Metaphysical Bookseller
Or Directly From Valley of the Sun Publishing

CONCENTRATION POWER PLUS
RX17® Audio Tape

Incorporates state-of-the-art digital recording and the latest brain/mind technology to synchronize both halves of your brain.

Example of Suggestions: You have the power and ability to focus your concentration at will. ■ Total concentration is yours when you want it. ■ You remain alert and focused on what you are doing. ■ You totally focus your concentration and energy at will. ■ You are a winner. ■ "Focus" is your key word for conditioned response.

.... RX126—$12.50

PAST-LIFE HYPNOTIC REGRESSION COURSE VOLUME I

Discover what past-life experiences influence, motivate and restrict you.

Contents: Tapes 1A & 1B: How To Receive In Regression; **Tape 2A:** A Door-Opening Regression; **Tape 2B:** Past-Life Regression To A Different Life; **Tape 3A:** Past-Life Involvement With Present Mate or Lover; **Tape 3B:** In-Depth Regression; **Tape 4A:** Karmic Investigation; **Tape 4B:** Regression Induction. Four tapes and instruction book in a vinyl album.

.... C801—$39.95

PAST-LIFE REGRESSION
RX17® Audio Tape

Contains a metaphysical induction that is ultra-powerful and totally enjoyable. Side One contains a basic introductory session in which you'll experience one of your past lifetimes. You can use the tape to explore a different incarnation with each use.

Once you are proficient with Side One, move on to the more advanced session on Side Two, which is a past-life regression that you direct. You decide what you want to explore; you can choose a different life each time you listen.

.... RX201—$12.50

HIGHER-SELF EXPLORATIONS

Tape 1: Transcendence: Achieving The Ultimate Level—A longer, expanded state-of-consciousness technique. **Tape 2: Verbal Channeling**—Establish contact with a highly evolved and friendly entity. **Tape 3: Direct Writing**—Induces an ultra-expanded state of consciousness. **Tape 4: Telepathic Contact On A Superconscious Level**—You will communicate directly through thought-to-thought transmission.

Two tapes and Instruction Manual.

.... C811—$24.95

Audio/Video Tapes That Relate To This Book
Available Through Your Local Metaphysical Bookseller
Or Directly From Valley of the Sun Publishing

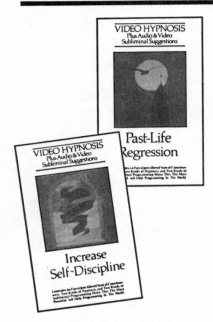

INCREDIBLE CONCENTRATION
Video Hypnosis®

Incredibly powerful four-way programming: visual hypnosis, verbal body relaxation and induction, and audio and video subliminals.

Examples of Suggestions: You now have the power and ability to focus your concentration at will. ■ Total concentration is yours whenever you want it. ■ You now focus your concentration and energy at will. ■ Every day in every way, you increase your ability to concentrate. ■ You can do anything you want to do. ■ You are a winner. You are a winner.

. . . . **VHS116—$19.95**

PAST-LIFE REGRESSION
Video Hypnosis®

Contains visual and verbal hypnosis, audio and video subliminals.

Examples of Suggestions: You can now perceive your past lives. ■ You trust your thoughts and fantasies. ■ Past-life awareness can release you. ■ Let the past-life impressions flow into your mind. ■ You have the ability to receive vivid impressions of your past lives. ■ You now let past-life impressions flow into your mind.

. . . . **VHS129—$19.95**

SELF-DISCIPLINE
Video Hypnosis®

Contains visual and verbal hypnosis, audio and video subliminals.

Examples of Suggestions: You now have the self-discipline you need to accomplish your personal and professional goals. ■ You direct your time and energy to manifest your desires. ■ Every day, you increase your self-discipline. ■ You do what you need to do to accomplish your goals and you stop doing what doesn't work.

. . . . **VHS147—$19.95**

Other Titles That Relate To This Book

Available Through Your Local Metaphysical Bookseller
Or Directly From Valley of the Sun Publishing

ENLIGHTENMENT TRANSCRIPTS

This book takes up where **Master of Life Manual** left off. Thirty-six fast-reading dialogues with processing sessions simplify complicated concepts and provide eye-opening, human-potential awareness through powerful examples of karma and past-life therapy.

Partial Contents: Science has proven that energy doesn't die, it simply transforms itself. • Unconditional love made workable and logical. • Sex and spirituality. • The three kinds of guilt and how to resolve them. • Sub-personalities. • And much, much more.

A 128-page paperback.

.... **B923—$3.95**

PAST-LIFE THERAPY IN ACTION

By Dick Sutphen & Lauren Leigh Taylor

Past-life therapy is becoming more commonly accepted, not only by the general population but by the brain/mind professionals as well. When your past-life subconscious programming is out of line with your present conscious desires, you will have undesirable effects.

The authors explore many exciting case histories and show the **cause, effect** and **karmic lesson,** providing human-potential awareness of how to rise above the effects.

Trade paperback; 144 pages.

.... **B915—$7.95**

Other Titles That Relate To This Book

Available Through Your Local Metaphysical Bookseller
Or Directly From Valley of the Sun Publishing

THE ORACLE WITHIN

The Oracle Within is a "magic" book that can provide you with answers, like the I Ching or Tarot cards, or it can be used as a self-actualization textbook. To consult this volume as an oracle, you need a clear and concise question. If you don't have a specific question, simply ask, "What do I most need to know at this time?" Close your eyes, breathe deeply and surround yourself with light. Dwell on the question for a moment, then open the book at random to read the message from your higher mind.

There are 250 message pages in the book, covering every aspect of metaphysical/human-potential philosophy. Some answers are direct; some provide you with awareness that you'll have to relate to your question.

At the end of each reading are instructions for further clarification. After you've read the next passage, you may toss the coin again for more clarification. (Don't ask for clarification more than three times.)

270 pages, large trade-size paperback.

. . . . **B909—$9.95**

Other Titles That Relate To This Book
Available Through Your Local Metaphysical Bookseller
Or Directly From Valley of the Sun Publishing

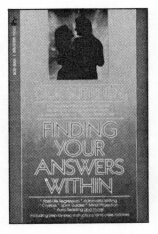

FINDING YOUR ANSWERS WITHIN

A complete manual for self-exploration and self-change.

The first section is on **Metaphysical Awareness & Techniques**. Chapters include spirit guides, past lives, parallel lives, automatic writing, psychometry, spiritual healing, group healing, crystals, mind projection (remote viewing) and the healing circle.

The second section of the book covers **Human-Potential Awareness & Techniques**. This information will enable you to effectively apply the metaphysical awareness in order to bring about practical change. Paperback.

.... B907—$4.50

EARTHLY PURPOSE

Sutphen unveils the heart of all his bestselling works and an incredible pact many of his readers may share.

Earthly Purpose is first a love story, and second, an in-depth exploration of the group reincarnation of 25,000 people who were once part of a highly advanced metaphysical civilization that existed in Mexico 1400 years ago. Dick combines known archeological facts with over 200 past-life regressions, Edgar Cayce readings, and psychic investigative techniques to tell the story. Half of the book is written in novelized docudrama style.

.... B908—$4.95

MAKE CHECKS PAYABLE TO
Valley of the Sun Publishing
Box 3004, Agoura Hills, CA 91376
818/889-1575

ORDER
FORM
RY2

Name

Address

City	State	Zip

Item Number	Name of Item	Qty.	Price

NO CASH OR C.O.D.'S PLEASE

Prices subject to change without notice. Offers in other Valley of the Sun catalogs do not relate to any items offered here. VISA and MasterCard orders, call toll-free: 1-800-421-6603.

CANADIAN—Please include $7.50 extra in U.S. funds.
FOREIGN—Please write for a PRO FORMA invoice.

MERCHANDISE TOTAL	
CA SALES TAX (Residents only, 8.25%)	
SHIPPING CHARGE	$3.00
ORDER TOTAL	

■■■■■■■■■■■■■■■■■■■■■■■■■■■■■■■■■■

MAKE CHECKS PAYABLE TO
Valley of the Sun Publishing
Box 3004, Agoura Hills, CA 91376
818/889-1575

ORDER
FORM
RY2

Name

Address

City	State	Zip

Item Number	Name of Item	Qty.	Price

NO CASH OR C.O.D.'S PLEASE

Prices subject to change without notice. Offers in other Valley of the Sun catalogs do not relate to any items offered here. VISA and MasterCard orders, call toll-free: 1-800-421-6603.

CANADIAN—Please include $7.50 extra in U.S. funds.
FOREIGN—Please write for a PRO FORMA invoice.

MERCHANDISE TOTAL	
CA SALES TAX (Residents only, 8.25%)	
SHIPPING CHARGE	$3.00
ORDER TOTAL	